To Roger.
Best wishes.

MOUNTAINS

of the

MOON

LUNAR NIGHTS ON
SCOTLAND'S HIGH PEAKS

Alan Rowan

ALAN ROWAN

BACKPAGE

First published in Great Britain in 2019.
This edition published 2019 by
BACKPAGE

www.backpagepress.co.uk
@BackPagePress

Copyright © Alan Rowan

ISBN: 9781909430389
eBook ISBN: 9781909430396

A catalogue record for this book is available on request
from the British Library.

Typeset by BackPage
Cover design by Chris Hannah
Printed in Great Britain by MBM Print

For the girls –

Alison, Claire, Lucy, Ava, Lily and Amber

Full Moons 2018

Wolf Moon (January 2)
Packs of wolves were heard howling in hunger as food became scarce at the end of winter. Also sometimes known as the Old Moon.

Blue Moon (January 31)
When two moons appear in the same month, the second is called a blue moon. Had the moon risen one day later in February it would have been the Snow Moon, also sometimes referred to as the Hunger Moon.

Worm Moon (March 2)
As the temperatures start to rise, the ground begins to thaw and earthworms make their way to the surface providing a feast for birds. Also known as the Sap Moon, Crow Moon and Lenten Moon.

Blue Moon (March 31)
The second blue moon of the year – an event that only happens roughly every 20 years. The next blue moon will be October 31, 2020.

Pink Moon (April 30)
It's not the moon itself which turns pink but the ground, which is carpeted in wildflowers. Also sometimes called the Egg Moon due to the spring egg-laying season or the Fish Moon.

Flower Moon (May 29)
Spring has officially arrived by May and flowers and colourful blooms are in abundance on the landscape. This moon is also known as Corn Planting Moon, Milk Moon or Mother's Moon.

Strawberry Moon (June 28)
This moon is named after the beginning of the strawberry picking season. Other names are Rose Moon, Hot Moon or Hay Moon as hay is typically harvested at this time.

Buck Moon (July 27)
This is the time when a buck or stag's antlers will be fully grown. Often referred to as the Thunder Moon due to the prevalence of summer thunderstorms.

Sturgeon Moon (August 26)
The rivers would be rich with fish at this time and the tribes could catch them by moonlight. Grain and corn were gathered at this time hence the other name, Grain Moon.

Harvest Moon (September 25)

The light of this moon enabled farmers to work longer into the evening to harvest their crops. Some tribes also called it the Barley Moon or Corn Moon. The Harvest Moon can sometimes occur in October, whichever moon is closest to the autumnal equinox.

Hunter's Moon (October 24)

The light of this bright moon made it easy for hunters to spot prey ahead of the lean winter months. It's also called Blood Moon.

Beaver Moon (November 23)

The winter frosts began to take their toll and the tribes set their traps to gather for food and furs before the lakes froze over. Also known sometimes as the Frost Moon.

Cold Moon (December 22)

As winter's grip tightens, nights are long and dark so this last moon of the year is sometimes the only light. Also referred to as Moon Before Yule and Long Nights Moon.

Chinese full moon names:

January – Holiday Moon
February – Budding Moon
March – Sleepy Moon
April – Peony Moon
May – Dragon Moon
June – Lotus Moon
July – Hungry Ghost Moon
August – Harvest Moon
September – Chrysanthemum Moon
October – Kindly Moon
November – White Moon
December – Bitter Moon

Celtic full moon names:

January – Quiet Moon
February – Moon of Ice
March – Moon of Winds
April – Growing Moon
May – Bright Moon
June – Moon of Horses
July – Moon of Calming
August – Dispute Moon
September – Singing Moon
October – Harvest Moon
November – Dark Moon
December – Cold Moon

Mountains of the Moon

It sounded simple enough: 13 moons, 13 mountains. An iconic Scottish peak on every night of a full moon in an exceptional year of full moons.

A year in which there were 13 full moons instead of the usual 12. A year in which there was no full moon in February. A year in which we had not one, but two, blue moons. It only happens four or five times each century, roughly every 19 years. It hasn't happened since 1999 and won't happen again until 2037.

I would choose a mountain that reflected the name of that specific moon, and each time and date was set in stone. After all, this is the moon we're talking about, not a rail timetable. No excuses, no moon running late because there are leaves cluttering its path or the wrong type of moonbeams.

But I walk in Scotland, home of the contrary weather

system. It's a lot to ask for favourable conditions on 13 specific dates in the mountains, some would say impossible. When you factor in aiming at one particular mountain on each of these nights, the odds diminish further to somewhere south of winning the lottery and then riding in on the Loch Ness Monster to collect your winnings.

I hoped there would be some sensational nights; long, lazy walking, a constant rising in beautiful light on moonlit slopes to a summit cairn to wait for the sun to arrive for a new beginning. I hoped to juggle the timing of each walk as much as the parameters allowed to catch either a sunset, the full moon or a cracking sunrise. All three would be nice, but you can't get too greedy.

I knew there would likely be snow and gales and heavy rain. There would be nights where climbing a mountain would be regarded by some as foolish, even dangerous. I was ready for extreme conditions, but only to a point. I would not put my life at risk, nor that of anyone else. Mountain rescue teams are there to help those who desperately need it: they can do without anyone stupidly putting themselves in harm's way. If conditions got too bad, I would bale out.

If I managed to summit my chosen Munro and make it back down safely I would be happy. Anything else would be a bonus. I knew it was odds-on I would not get the perfect 13; one failure would be acceptable, two would be pushing it. Any more and the plug would be pulled on the whole project.

It meant a year of weather watching, a constant eye to the skies. I would always be on the look-out for weather windows, those soothing moments between the storms. The ascents had to be on the day or night of each particular full moon, so a few hours' respite could be the key to success. I could time it so I avoided the wilder weather blasting over the higher regions, setting off in the rain and wind, watching it blow itself out and clear as I rose.

It would provide a fascinating snapshot of a year in the Scottish mountains; through the increasing and then decreasing length of the days, the changing of the seasons, the variations in weather patterns, the cycles of plant and animal life.

It would also be interesting to see how I would cope physically and mentally with being a noctivagant again on a regular basis. I started my night ascents in 1994 when I was working back shifts on newspapers in Glasgow. Long days and irregular hours meant my mountain time was limited so I took to starting my walks after midnight when my shift finished. The early outings were a revelation and this became a habit. It remained so until I retired in 2009. Over those 16 years, I had climbed some 300 mountains in the wee, small hours, racking up the best part of two rounds of Munros and one of Corbetts.

My new, more relaxed, phase of life meant there was no pressing need to go out at night, but after six months off I found I missed it; I missed watching the setting sun amidst flame-red and fiery orange skies, missed starting a walk by moonlight, missed rising with the day, missed sitting on a high summit enjoying breakfast with not another soul around. The torches came out again, and the night walks continued. The difference this time was that I was far choosier in my targets. It wasn't a case of going out every week, instead I would go when conditions were perfect, long traverses in the Cairngorms and the Fisherfields, often on assignment for magazine articles, sometimes for mountain festivals. The over-riding factor was that I always had options. This new project would change all that. Now I had to stick rigidly to set dates and times.

The one consolation was that there was a little leeway on the choice of mountains. I picked mountains whose name matched each particular full moon. I decided at the outset that the main mountain had to be a Munro, a Scottish mountain over 3,000ft, named after Sir Hugh Munro who compiled the original list in 1891. This would limit choice; sometimes there would be smaller hills that were a more comfortable fit, but I wanted to stick to a self-imposed set of guidelines rather than randomly change with each climb.

All the main mountain areas would be covered; Skye, Torridon, Cairngorms, Lochaber, Affric and Knoydart, with a finish on the most northerly Munro, Ben Hope. I would try to find a couple of mountain choices for each walk, ideally one in the east, the other in the west. This would mean I could switch tack at the last minute and head for the more favourable conditions.

Sometimes the names of the moon and the peak correlated perfectly. For instance, Cairn Gorm, the blue mountain, and the Blue Moon.

Sometimes, it might be a feature of a specific mountain that matched such as Toll a' Mhadaidh Mor, the big hollow of the dog (wolf) on Beinn Alligin for the Wolf Moon.

On the odd occasion when there was nothing that directly matched, it was a case of picking a mountain that invoked something like a specific method of travel or nearby location or event that best linked the name of the moon.

These were my rules and these were my Mountains of the Moon.

Each of the chosen mountains would have to be climbed on the actual date of the full moon as it fell in Scotland, even if that meant just a matter of minutes after midnight. There were a few options.

For instance, if the full moon fell here at 00.51am on

the 26th of the month, the ideal scenario would be to start climbing as soon as the clock ticked past midnight, and I could spend most of the night on the hill and sit and wait to drink in the sunrise.

If the weather conditions weren't ideal, I could ascend during the evening of the 25th, so long as I was on the hill at some point during the 26th. And if the inclemency was more extreme, I could set off around 4am to catch the moon and come down in the light.

The moons that reached their fullest during the middle of a day gave the best options; I had the luxury of choosing from the two nights on either side.

The big get-out in all this – short of calling it off altogether – was to accept when it seemed impossible or downright suicidal to be on the hill on the requisite date, and go up instead the night before or the night after. This would be a last resort, to be used sparingly. If it was getting to be a habit, then again I would call a halt to the whole thing.

Most of my early night walking had been a solo affair, and on the odd occasion I did have company not many came back for seconds. This project seemed to have stirred the imagination, however, and I was keen to have a variety of guests along. The romance of the idea was undoubtable, and I had plenty of enquiries and notes of interest, but when it came to the reality of setting off up a mountain in the middle of the night, that list was quickly whittled down.

Many cultures have their own names for the full moons but I had based my mountain names on the full moons that have been adopted from the Native American tribes. It is also based on our use of the Gregorian calendar – named after Pope Gregory XIII who introduced it in 1582.

The tribes didn't record time using the months of that calendar, but instead gave each full moon a nickname to keep track of the seasons and lunar months. These names relate to an activity or an event that took place at those times, and they were adopted by the colonial Americans. These are:

January – Wolf Moon
February – Snow Moon
March – Worm Moon
April – Pink Moon
May – Flower Moon
June – Strawberry Moon
July – Buck Moon
August – Sturgeon Moon
September – Harvest Moon
October – Hunter's Moon
November – Beaver Moon
December – Cold Moon

Many tribes named and counted moons differently. Some, for instance, counted four seasons a year while others counted five. Some defined a year as 12 moons, others 13. One name might be used by some for a certain month, others might gift it to a different month. For the sake of continuity, I stuck to the names used specifically by the Algonquian tribes.

A full moon is seen when the moon is on the opposite side of the Earth from the sun. It means the moon, sun and Earth are in line with the Earth between the sun and the moon. When that happens the whole surface of the moon appears to be illuminated.

A new moon refers to the moment when the moon is between the Earth and the sun, and we see the opposite side of the moon on which the sun shines. At that point, the moon is too close to the sun for us to see it at all.

Each full cycle of the moon lasts 29.53 days, and is made up of eight phases: New Moon, Waxing Crescent, First Quarter, Waxing Gibbous, Full Moon, Waning Gibbous, Last Quarter, Waning Crescent.

The word gibbous refers to a bulging or convex shape, and derives from the Latin gibbus, meaning hump-backed. A gibbous moon is when the illuminated part is greater than a half-moon yet less than a full moon.

There are typically 12 full moons each year, one for each month, but roughly every two and a half years, a 13th full moon is seen. This additional moon doesn't fit into the normal naming scheme and is referred to as a blue moon.

The correct definition of a blue moon is that it is the third full moon in an astronomical season containing four full moons (a season usually has three), but it has become common (and simpler) to explain a blue moon as being the second full moon to fall in the same month. In 2018, February had no full moon while January and March had two each, so by this second definition both these months contained blue moons.

To confuse things further, different parts of the globe and different time zones may not experience the same number or position of blue moons in any year because the moon has only one moment when it is full and it might not be visible from all these points.

Once in a blue moon is a saying that has come to be used to denote an unusual event, such as finding a seat on a train or Donald Trump putting together a coherent sentence. Two blue moons in any one year is even more unusual, an event that only happens every 20 years or so. It won't happen again until 2037 so I had to make this work in 2018 – I doubt that as an 83-year-old I would be able to make up lost time 19 years from now.

Blue moons can happen in any month which contains 31 days – the next one is on October 20, 2020 – but when there are two blue moons in a year, they tend to fall in January and March. February is always the fall guy because it is the only month which has fewer days than the full moon cycle of 29.53 days.

It's unclear where the term 'blue moon' originated but one theory is that it may be a mispronunciation of an old word 'belewe' which means to betray. This could be a reference to the 'betrayal' by the moon of worshippers trying to determine the timing and duration of Lent in the calendar year. When there is no full moon in a month, the term 'black moon' has increasingly slipped into common usage.

To this lunar mix, I decided to add two other factors – music and alcohol. Music plays a massive part in helping pass the time of long night drives, and it has been a staple of every walk, day or night. Just as certain songs trigger memories in any walk of life, my mountain treks always have a piece of music running through them, deliberately or otherwise.

My taste is wide and varied. I can listen to pop, heavy metal, rap and classical all in the same journey. Nothing is off limits, so each mountain and each moon pairing also has a theme tune. Some have titles or lyrics that match the name of the moon, some match the name of the mountain. Some are obvious, some totally left field. Some I knew well, some I rediscovered after years of silence, some I stumbled across during the research for the book. And some were just earworms, ideas that I looked at, listened to and then discovered I couldn't get them out of my head.

The same applied to alcohol. The new drink-drive limits in Scotland have drastically changed the culture over the past few years. It used to be that everyone went for a pint after coming off the hill. Now, it tends to be straight home unless you are travelling by train or coach. But I wanted to toast every successful ascent in this new venture, so I conducted considerable research (ie. I drank a lot) into different drinks that again summed up the moon or the mountain. It was quaff a minute stuff at times, but the result was a decent selection of music and drinks for every occasion.

I had my moon, my mountain, my soundtrack and my celebratory tipple for every occasion. Hopefully, I would also have some company. Now I just had to get and climb on every one of those 13 nights.

1
Howling at the Moon

WOLF MOON

(Tuesday, January 2, 02.24)
Mountain: *Beinn Alligin (Toll a' Mhadaidh Mhor)*
Soundtrack: *The Wolf and the Moon – Brunuhville*
Celebratory drink: *Wolf Warning (Swedish lager)*

IT'S 5am on January 2nd and I'm standing high on Beinn Alligin howling at the moon. This is the Wolf Moon, the first full moon of the year, but the perfect shining orb which has illuminated upward progress on this massive Torridon mountain has just vanished.

Dominant for the first stretch of the ascent through pavements of sandstone, it has been gradually weakened by gathering cloud until it is a muted, throbbing light surrounded by circles of many colours equally faded by superior forces. Minute by minute its influence wanes, overwhelmed by thick layers of gauze, until it is just a pinprick, a failing torch in a sea of darkness.

As I head higher into the mouth of Coir nan Laogh, the

last vestige of light disappears, blocked by the imposing buttress of Na Fasreidhnean which forms the protecting left-hand wall of the corrie.

Suddenly, the darkness seems absolute. The temperature drops several degrees, and, to serve as a timely reminder that this is the middle of a freezing winter night, it starts to snow.

The only visibility is to the lower slopes of the soaring white corrie walls, rising in a sweep into nothingness, laden with menace. For the first time, I am acutely aware that I am alone in this wild place and everything has just become much more threatening.

The corrie ahead is shaped like a Venus fly-trap. My mind conjures up images of strolling in there and setting off a hair-trigger that causes it to snap closed, cutting escape.

I make a decision; I will not push on. I will not attempt to climb these walls with the threat of avalanche hanging over me. I will not try to reach the summit of Tom na Gruagaich. That is not the main point of this walk. Although it would have been satisfying to climb on to the main ridge and circuit this leviathan with the full moon throbbing beatifically overhead, the rapidly changing conditions have produced a change in circumstance.

I switch to Plan B, and the real mission, the exploration of Toll a' Mhadaidh Mor, the big hollow of the dog (it can also mean fox or wolf). This huge corrie fills the vast horseshoe which runs from the floor under Tom na Gruagaich, curving round the plunging slopes of the main summit of Sgurr Mhor and the great notch of Eag Dhubh, the 'black cleft', before following the line of the triple-topped pinnacles of Na Rathanan, the Horns of Alligin. But before I descend into the snows and shadows of this vast amphitheatre there's something I have to do: I throw my head back and howl into the night skies.

After all, this was the night of the Wolf Moon, and legend has it that one of the last wolves was hunted down to its lair in this corrie and killed along with its cubs. I wanted to head into this corrie on this night and explore by moonlight. And, of course, like any wolf worth its salt, howl at the moon.

As part of the build-up, I had remained unshaven for a few days, but I hadn't gone full lycanthrope. This was as hairy as it was going to get for this production of A Dundonian Werewolf in Torridon. It's not likely there would be any competition; I was certain I would be the lone wolf here.

I stood howling for a few minutes with the light snow driving into my face, slightly disappointed but not surprised there was no answering cry. The wolf has long disappeared from our landscape, and, despite the push for a re-introduction in many quarters, I suspect it will remain merely the dream of the romantic. There are just far too many barriers to setting loose an apex predator in these modern times.

I feel I should apologise, however, to anyone who might have been in the vicinity. I would imagine it would have invoked a shiver down the spine to hear howls coming from the mountain, especially to any red-cloaked small child carrying a picnic basket to her granny as a first foot.

The route across the corrie took a while, the need for care in picking my way over the undulating ground in direct contrast to the simple steps of the path. The snow had ceased but the wind was picking up, a prelude to a front approaching from the west that would bring heavy rain driven in by fierce winds, another reason I was glad to be under, rather than on, the crest of the mountain.

The Eag Dhubh looked particularly striking in the

burgeoning light, its black slash slicing through vertical bookends of white, but the arriving morning was disappointing. The hoped-for sunrise was a mere blink of yellow on the eastern horizon which failed to filter through the gloom, losing the battle between east and west. The consolation was making it back to base before the rain swept in.

I may have failed to reach the summits of the jewelled mountain, but I had spent a few hours in the company of the first full moon of the year. This was the first of the 13 planned for this year. Beinn Alligin was the rock from which this project would be launched. It was also the rock on which the whole thing could founder. My grand plans could come crashing to a premature halt if I failed to make it out at the first time of asking.

The groundwork had been laid weeks and even months before but as the day drew closer, the doubts started to surface. I had arranged the use of the Grampian Club's cottage in Torridon, a perfect base for the unpredictable hours involved. The climb was very much weather dependent.

The forecast was relatively calm after a few days of sometimes storm force winds and heavy snow, but these were the long dark nights of January and I would be heading up to try to catch the Wolf Moon at its prime, 2.24am. There was also the condition of the roads to take into account – Torridon is a long drive from home.

§

IT felt strange to be leaving the New Year celebrations and the company of family and friends and heading off alone into the night, even though I've never held any affection for Hogmanay and its attendant revelries. Indeed, it is a time of year I have always loathed. I could happily go into hibernation after Christmas and not come out again for a couple of weeks when all the fake celebrations and amateur drinkers are packed away until the next time. I often did. I would volunteer to work over the New Year period, giving me the perfect excuse to avoid the seemingly never-ending parties when so many enjoy the challenge of trying to trump everyone else on how long they can go without sleep while constantly topping up their alcohol level to staggering levels.

It has been a trauma for as long as I can remember. As a child living in a Dundee housing scheme, I dreaded the moment when my parents started laying out the contents of the drinks cabinet 'just in case' we had visitors. And when the Bells tolled, it was if they were tolling for me, a signal that mayhem was about to enter through the front door.

Leaving the house lights on seemed a provocation, an invitation to anyone passing that the bar was open and that there was no limit on last orders.

Right on cue they arrived, the decibel count rising to the level where it sounds as if everyone is spoiling for a fight. One couple, Wullie and Mary, were regulars, but it was the only time of year we would be honoured by their company. At other times, they were heard but not really seen, Wullie fancying himself as a low-rent Sinatra, belting out songs outside the window every weekend after being thrown out of the pub. They were like the warring shop couple in Father Ted, constantly looking for any perceived slight, belittling and insulting each other through a range of slurred curses.

For a child, this lurched into Stephen King territory; the garishly painted faces and smudged lipstick of these harpies, soaked in a perfume overload and smelling as though they had washed their hair in a bucket of gin, the dishevelled males all manic arm gestures and creepy asides, spilling and swilling and growling like cavemen. Even when we were able to escape to the hoped-for calm of our bedrooms, it proved to be a far from soundproof sanctuary, the noise rising from downstairs still a constant anxiety.

My teenage years did little to win back Hogmanay. Peer pressure meant heading to the centre of town whatever the weather to join the mobs pretending to be all things to all men and women for the five minutes either side of the Bells before reverting to type and the usual hostilities. Guys who earlier that evening were trying to pan your head in suddenly became your best pal. Ten minutes later, they would be trying to stab you to jump the taxi queue. When the chimes struck the roar went up and then there was a five-minute window for every randy teen to try to kiss as many members of the opposite sex as possible. This was a mass orgy Eskimo-style, 15 layers of impenetrable clothes that reduced everyone to the same vital statistics, safety in layers.

The pleasant surprise of a successful no-strings attached snog with a stranger proved scant consolation when the realisation hit that you were miles from home with no transport. What followed was a less starry-eyed version of *The Warriors*; the trawl round the streets looking for sanctuary at a party that usually didn't exist as everyone else was out doing the same, the fake bravado of staying away from home as long as possible for the bragging contest that would inevitably take up the next few days when the true inclination would have been to find a warm bed.

On the rare occasion you did make it home and crashed out, there was the rude awakening with the panicked thought that maybe, just maybe, you may have mistaken the kitchen sink for the toilet (it happened) followed by the desperate silent dash to destroy the evidence before your mum and dad went to make breakfast.

With memories like these, it's no wonder that in more mature times I have been more than happy to give the whole thing a body-swerve. Dry January has been a recurring fixture with me for years. After the Christmas parties, I went teetotal for a month or two. Nothing to do with detox or starting the new year with a healthy outlook. I just preferred to avoid the amateurs, the ones who feel they have a duty to indulge at this time, packing out the pubs and disturbing the regulars. There's an overload of delusory nostalgia. If you want to enjoy the traditions of the music, the dancing and the whisky, go for it. Just don't expect me to join in.

§

TO say the days building up to this first outing were fraught would be an understatement. My overriding thought was the project could go south before it had even started. Weather forecasts had been changing by the minute. First we had settled conditions in Torridon. A couple of days later there was the threat of gales and heavy snow. The avalanche threat had risen, not something you want to hear when heading into an enclosed corrie with steep, loaded walls. The SAIS forecast site became a much-used favourite, and the Torridon Mountain Rescue team provided me with up to the minute advice on the conditions.

There was constant turmoil in my mind. One minute I was going with one plan. The next I was having doubts and looking at other options. But Scottish weather is so localised, and in the end there was only one way to find out the best way to go – I had see for myself.

Timing would be vital, but with the target mountain some four and a half hours away, it was proving difficult to judge. There was no point in heading up too early. The weather wasn't clearing until late evening on the 1st and the thought of getting there and then having to sit it out at the side of the road in a freezing glen for hour upon hour didn't particularly appeal.

Access to the club cottage wouldn't kick in until midday on the 2nd as other guests were already in situ for the New Year celebrations. There was the added complication of a fierce frontal system heading in around 9am. I wanted to be off the hill by then. I eventually figured that as long as I was ready to go on the mountain just after midnight, I would have a chance of catching the moon at its fullest.

The first signs were good. As I was scraping the ice from my car, the moon made its first full appearance, a massive, pulsating, perfect circle hovering above the beach and sending out bright white beams on to the cold waters of the North Sea. I began to have visions of this wonderful disco ball sparkling on the slopes of Beinn Alligin as if placed on the razor's edge by careful hands.

It stayed in my rearview mirror all the way through the deserted streets of Dundee, then past Perth and up the A9 to Pitlochry. The threat of icy roads had not materialised and it felt like a summer's evening drive. The first signs of a change happened around Drumochter. Here on the higher part of the road, snow was banked up on the verges, and the pure whiteness of the surrounding land combined with more cloud cover implied a huge temperature drop. The journey was still ticking past nicely, the miles being helped along with my private Little Feat festival, a five-album stress-buster with Lowell George and Co providing the ideal cruising mood.

Just after Aviemore the journey changed. During all my years of night ascents, it was the travelling that put me off more than the climbing. I was confident enough on the mountains in winter conditions but reaching them was a bigger worry, the unpredictability of snow and ice-covered roads, especially along the minor offshoots for access points to the chosen hill. This invariably would be the reason to abandon walking plans rather than the condition on the mountain.

I had been cruising along nicely when the car hit a patch of black ice, skidded right then back left before I got it under control. The caution button had been well and truly pushed and I reduced my speed to a crawl. Even with the security blanket provided by snow tyres my confidence had been shaken. From here on in, running times would be affected.

I drove through the icy mist congregating in the dip that houses Inverness to emerge into a different world, a constant plummeting of the temperature all the way along the rutted road through the trees to Garve. The red figures on the dash kept dropping: minus three, four, five, six, seven. Then I turned towards Achnasheen and winter gripped. The moon had long disappeared, but the road still shone a wet black with innumerable pinpricks of light reflecting from the headlights, as if millions of diamonds had been crushed, scattered and steamrollered into the surface. My speed was 20mph tops, every bend approached with trepidation. My arms were feeling the strain of gripping the wheel so I decided to take a break in the layby at Loch a' Chuilinn.

This is a favourite stopping point. In the winter months there is often an icy mist sitting low on the loch while the sun shines above. Tonight there was only sheet ice on the ground and a feeling that the sky was also filled with the same. There was one other occupant, a camper van parked up for the night. I hope they had good heating. That was one of the surprising factors of the journey so far – the number of cars and campers parked at Munro starting points all the way up the road. It seems I was not the only one desperate to escape the New Year over-indulgence.

The new ice age of the last 20 miles or so had me fearing the worst; that Beinn Alligin was an impossibility, that the minor road to the foot of the walk would prove treacherous, its ice-coated surface a certain passage off the road and into the trees. Combined with the missing moon, I entertained thoughts of turning round and finding a mountain further south which would at least give me the moonlight if not the wolf connection. I could howl at the moon from any high point. But when I reached the road split at Achnasheen, conditions changed again. As I dropped towards Kinlochewe, the roadside snow diminished and numbers on the dash started climbing again. By the time I was in Glen Torridon, it was positively balmy. The downside to this was a cloudier sky: this moon was playing hard to get. The high tops of Beinn Eighe and Liathach were hidden, but the snow on their lower slopes looked skeletal, bones of white on a dark backdrop. Upper Loch Torridon was an uninviting grey metallic sheet.

I reached the Coire Mhic Nobuil car park without any problem, the plus temperature and the sheltered nature of its route keeping it clear. It was 1am and there was no sign of the main attraction or Beinn Alligin. They were both up there somewhere: I just had to wait for them to reappear. I began to consider my options. I knew I had a window, but I would have to get going soon. My first choice route wasn't looking promising, so I pondered other options.

I decided to make the short drive a few miles further west to the high point of the road to see if that offered better prospects. From there, I could make the short climb to the small but beautifully formed An Ruadh-mheallan, drop off the back and then traverse round the back of Beinn Alligin, taking in the wonderfully named Toll nam Biast, the 'hollow of the beast', before swinging round and out by the Coire Mhic Nobuil path. But there's a lot of complicated ground to cross, and if the moon never made it back out, it would be a dark and dicey circuit, so I nixed that idea and headed back to the car park.

For once on this expedition, my timing was right. As I pulled in, the car park was suddenly floodlit. The moon was back out to play, and Beinn Alligin was visible. I put on the requisite layers, and set off on the rocky contoured path, the head torch redundant in a light that would have cheered many a summer day.

The Wolf Moon was on the rise, the only blip the fuzzy rainbow halos spreading out in pulses around it. This is said to be a portent of wet or stormy weather, not just for the immediate future but for the whole year. A bright first moon is said to be a harbinger of wet weather and a good harvest while one with a red tinge spells a dry year. This one had a touch of all three so the jury is out, but if I were a betting man, I would go for the first option. A wet and stormy year in Scotland? That's like putting a wager on a bear's preferential toilet area.

As I rose through the rock terraces in the perfect light, I encountered more snow, deeper with every few metres of ascent until the path was lost. The illumination was still good enough to follow the best line towards the corrie, but I could feel it starting to dim, the cold starting to nip. The moon was becoming increasingly fuzzy, a satellite losing its signal like an old-fashioned television set, the picture dimming and fading. Its power was diminishing fast, the light being hoovered up from the land as the cloud closed in. With the light went the illusion of warmth, the temperature dipping fast. Then I became aware of the snow, light but disturbing nonetheless, as it seemed to have sneaked up unnoticed under the false blanket of security I had had so far. For the first time, this felt like a winter night, dark and cold, and when a few more steps onward took me into the shadow of the buttress and out of the moonlight, any lingering doubt of the serious nature of this trek disappeared.

Now I had a choice – enter the dragon's den and head up into the unknown, or pick my way carefully among the undulations of the snow-covered heather and boulders into the hollow of the wolf. The wolf was the main feature so the decision was made, and after a spot of howling at the now invisible moon I set off into the corrie.

§

THE Beinn Alligin wolf legend is just one of many in Scotland. The last wolf is often said to have been killed at the River Findhorn in 1743, hunted down after allegedly attacking a woman and her children.

Wolves were part of the natural fauna from about 50,000 years ago until the middle of the 18th century. Their bones have been found, along with those of reindeer, lynx, bear and arctic fox, in caves at Inchnadamph in Sutherland, and in Ayrshire.

Early hunters respected and revered the wolf as a creature of powerful magical and spiritual properties, but the increasing rise of farming lifestyles radically altered this relationship. The clearing of wolf habitat led to displacement and the resultant shortages of wild prey meant the wolf became a nuisance to farmers. This conflict is recorded as far back as the 2nd century BC when a king called Dorvadilla decreed that any man slaying a wolf would be rewarded with an ox.

There is little evidence of wolf attacks on humans, although there are accounts of wolves feasting on dead bodies on battlefields and they had a tendency to dig up buried corpses. This habit made the wolf feared and despised. Christians saw it as a personification of the Devil, desecrating consecrated ground and devouring human souls. There's a tradition from Ederachillis in Sutherland that the dead had to be buried on the island of Handa to preserve them being disinterred by wolves.

Wolf persecution continued relentlessly from the 13th century. James I passed an Act for the destruction of wolves with hunts to be carried out three times a year, between St Mark's Day (April 25) and Lammas (August 1) when cubs were born. One hunt during the reign of Mary, Queen of Scots, was said to have killed five wolves.

But this persecution had little effect on the general population; it was the destruction of the forests rather than hunting which finally brought the wolf to the brink of extinction.

During James V's time, large tracts of Scotland were covered in forests of pine, birch, oak and other tree species, from Inverness-shire to Perthshire, Ardgour to Rannoch Moor. These heavily wooded areas provided a refuge for the animals, and it was not until large-scale felling and burning of these native woodlands that the wolf began the road to extinction. Large areas were destroyed at the end of the 16th and beginning of the 17th centuries. Heavy logging for shipbuilding and other industries further devastated the spread.

There is a growing cry for wolves to be re-introduced to Scotland, but the opposition is fierce. The romantic in me thinks it would be wonderful, the realist thinks it unlikely. Seeing humankind's unblinking propensity for cruelty and disregard for anything outside of the norm, I fear that unless legislation was in place to protect the wolf, it would only become persecuted again.

§

I EMERGED wearily from the corrie in a dim light with hopes that I might at least catch a glowing sunrise, and sat down by the bridge over the Abhainn Coire Mhic Nobuil in anticipation. But the western forces were massing, the breeze was picking up and the smell of rain was in the air. When the first sign of morning started to peer between Beinn Dearg and Beinn Eighe it was a muted affair, the colour scheme flat and listless leaving a monochrome wash over the dark walls and water all around. Even the grand slash of the Eag Dubh looked subdued.

I reached the car just as the rain delivered its promise, and drove round to the deserted front at Shieldaig to wait out the few hours before I could get access to the cottage. I watched one of the island's resident sea eagles circling its territory, its peaceful, dreamlike movement proving more effective than counting sheep and I soon nodded off. The increasing ferocity of the driven rain on the windshield woke me not long after, the car shaking with the incoming gusts.

I drove back towards Torridon, Beinn Alligin hidden in the overwhelming grey, and was relieved to discover the occupants of the cottage had departed. Now I could truly wind down after the stress of the last 24 hours, the anxious planning, the long drive, the dark hours of decision-making on the mountain. And yet I couldn't. The sleep pattern had been disrupted, and the best thing now was to stay awake until early evening and then try to ease back into normality.

I've been night walking for some 25 years, but this felt different from the early days. Then I was bounding up mountains after midnight and six hours later driving back to Glasgow to begin another shift at work. More recently, I have been choosing perfect nights and the walks have been more relaxed, the pressure eased. But having a fixed set of dates and targets was going to be so much more difficult. There's no opt-out, no waiting for better spells of weather, no waiting to feel in peak condition. Everything is immediate. I have to make do with what is there. And if I fail to make the grade with one walk, there's the chance the whole lot comes to an inglorious halt.

There's a growing feeling inside that this is a younger person's game, that I've cheated my age to sneak in and take part. It all felt so good 20 years ago; now it's a major consideration. I'm just another fading contestant on the Aches Factor.

I slept long and late. And as luck would have it, the moon produced its finest display for days over Beinn Alligin early the following morning, generating pink, blue and violet layers from the lying snow. By the time we were on the path round into Coire Mhic Fhearchair a few hours later it had long vanished, leaving behind a day of snow showers and occasional light relief. The views over the winterised Flowerdale peaks and lochs were achingly beautiful, bathed in every shade and tone of light, but that was as good as it got and the Triple Buttress remained shrouded in mist.

There was one surprise left. Around midnight, and with the cottage in darkness, I went through to kitchen to be greeted by the sight that had so far eluded me over the past few days. Here was mighty Liathach, its long wall stretched across the horizon dwarfing the lights of the tiny houses beneath, lit perfectly by the moon, snow-streaked and majestic, and topped by a clear sky filled with stars. I went outside into the icebox to soak up this rare show of perfection. Torridon had finally delivered. I may have missed the moon for the best part of my night on Beinn Alligin, but this re-awakened an optimism that the best was yet to come on this long moon walk.

2
The White Darkness

BLUE MOON

(Wednesday, January 31, 13.26)
Mountain: *Cairn Gorm (Coire an t-Sneachda)*
Soundtrack: *Blue Moon – The Marcels*
Celebratory drink: *Blue Moon (Belgian wheat ale)*

If I'd had any doubts about how difficult it would be to correlate moon and mountain in perfect harmony then the mission to climb Cairn Gorm on January 31 drove it home with a sledgehammer.

It was the first Blue Moon of the year and I had chosen Cairn Gorm, the perfect mountain. Except it didn't turn out that way.

This was the second full moon to fall in January. It happens every two and a half years or so, but 2018 was particularly unusual because there were two blue moons, one in January and one in March. There was no full moon at all in February, the first time that has happened since 1999. It missed out by just one day. This Blue Moon was also a supermoon, as its closest proximity to Earth during its elliptical orbit made it appear larger, some seven per cent bigger and 15 per cent brighter than normal. And for the icing on the cake it was also a Blood Moon, courtesy of a reddish tinge which would be seen from certain parts of the globe.

Australia, Asia and some parts of the USA and Eastern Europe witnessed a lunar eclipse as the Earth passed between the sun and the moon, a perfect alignment of the three which hadn't happened for 152 years and won't again until 2028. The word 'blood' is used to describe the deep red colour of the sunlight that passes through our atmosphere to illuminate the moon. That red glow was produced by the same effect that gives us blue skies and red sunsets. So there you have it – a Super Blue Blood Moon.

Had it risen around 11 hours later, it would have fallen into the first day of February, and taken that month's usual name of Snow Moon.

Unfortunately, in Scotland we missed out on the full glory of this rare event, and some of us missed out on virtually on every aspect. There were some good, clear sightings of the moon in certain parts of the country at certain times, but it was haphazard and almost impossible to predict. We'll just have to be patient and look forward to the next spectacular.

There are other blue mountains – Carn Gorm in Glen Lyon and Bla Bheinn on Skye for instance – but Cairn Gorm was the one that had that extra factor. The correct name for the Cairngorms is the Monadh Ruadh, the red mountains, so that added the blood link into the mix. Then there's magnificent Coire an t-Sneachda, the corrie of the snows, a tip of the hat to the absent Snow Moon should the walk slide over into February.

I had pondered on the idea of waiting 24 hours to start the walk in the hope of more lenient conditions but that would be stretching my rules and the distinction in this case would be crucial. On many of the other full moon walks, I could better justify a switch, but this one meant moving from January into February, and there was no full moon due in this month. It would feel like cheating.

Besides, I wouldn't want to run the risk of sullying the beliefs of my Celtic ancestors. The first day of February was an important day on the calendar, Imbolc, the mid-point between the winter solstice and the spring equinox. It was also known as Candlemas or Feile Brighde, the quickening of the year, and it marks the Earth's awakening from the cold and the start of lambing.

It may have been marked on the calendar, but only the most optimistic of souls would recognise this as a change from the deep freeze. I pity the poor lambs who would be arriving into the world on this day of Arctic conditions. It felt a long way from any promise of spring.

I had it all figured out. Unfortunately, all these extra specifics only made the likelihood of success even more remote. Plan A was to summit Cairn Gorm, then stroll around the corrie rims with the moonlight lighting up the cornices. The weather put paid to that; high-level winds ranging from 35-50mph, strengthening to a possible 65 as the evening drew on, and frequent snow showers bringing white-out conditions.

The Cairn Gorm plateau is no place to be in zero visibility with the wind biting lumps out of you. These repeated blows drain energy with a frightening rapidity. Factor in deep snow preventing any consistency of footfall and the possibility of blindly straying too near the massive cornices hanging out into the unseen void like giant waves washing over the tops of plunging rock faces and it's a recipe for disaster.

In these winter climes, you should always have a Plan

B, and a Plan C, and D, as far up the alphabet as you care to go. Being a man of letters is a good bet for safety. I decided to approach through the Northern Corries with the option of going up top if conditions turned out better better than forecast.

§

IT didn't look welcoming on the journey up the A9. The forecast had shifted from promises of a clear night and benign conditions to heavy snow and gales over the space of just a few days. What had been planned with optimism had now taken on the mantle of fingers crossed and hope for the least worst. The thoughts of climbing on to the heights of Cairn Gorm in these conditions sent a shiver down my spine.

I was checking out the latest avalanche advice every hour or so. I was regularly looking at the Cairngorm Mountain cameras and I had contacted friends in Aviemore for updates on conditions on the roads and in the mountains.

At least the gear packing was simple; four under-layers, a down under-jacket and then full snow suit, winter warmth socks, heavy duty gloves, balaclava and thermal hat which would give me four levels of protection on the face and ears if needed. Helmet, crampons, ice axe, hot drink, cold drink, emergency shelter, enough food to last three days stranded in a car, a quilt and a pillow. And two head torches, a vital precaution for winter in the mountains.

I also brought along a couple of bottles of Blue Moon beer. It seems there were a lot of people buying into this moon adventure. My walking mate Robert had given me two bottles of this brew a few weeks ago in anticipation of this walk. A few days later, my wife Alison, not knowing about this present, turned up with another bottle of the same. A quick check online revealed that there is virtually a beer to match every full moon this year. This could get messy, a healthy pursuit being turned into a giant, lunar-led pub crawl. Just as well the walks are staggered.

The Blue Moon was packed in the rucksack. For artistic purposes only, you understand. A bottle of Blue Moon under a Blue Moon on the blue mountain. You can't blame a guy for trying. Although when I saw the latest weather forecast, I reckoned I might have been better staying in the house and downing all three offerings thereby saving myself a long drive.

The first message dropped just before I pulled out of the drive. Anne, from her home in Aviemore.

"Fine at the moment, just a light dusting of snow. Not icy, side roads are fine. But there are snow showers rattling through and it is very windy."

From my end, it was fine right up to Bruar. Then the grey swept in and the landscape vanished. With the snow right down to the road verges now, the recently planted seed of optimism faded fast.

The snow was falling heavier as Anne's next update came through.

"A few snow showers and roads are fine. Gorms have been clagged in all morning though and I don't know how the ski road is looking above Glenmore."

Ah yes, the ski road. Even with snow tyres on the car, the heavy snow had me wondering if it would be a folly trying to reach the top car park, and even more of a folly if I was coming down off the hill in the middle of the night only to find the snow gates shut.

I was debating whether I should cut my losses and head for somewhere likely to be more benign, a mountain with a simpler ascent and where there would be more chance of seeing the moon. Ben Vrackie came to mind, not much of a diversion. I also pondered the idea of heading to Glen Doll and somewhere like Broad Cairn. A full moon reflecting over the waters of Loch Muick would be spectacular.

But I kept going, mainly because I was just 20 minutes from Aviemore and I had time on my hands. I would head in and check the lie of the land. I reckoned as long as the ski road was clear I would give it a go. If it was becoming too unforgiving I could turn tail and head back down to the simpler delights of Ben Vrackie.

A final, somewhat ominous, message from Anne: "Good luck." I would need that and a lot more.

Welcome shafts of sunlight were piercing the boiling white and grey blanket overhead and lighting up Loch Morlich, the small islands of vegetation sparkling in the silvery wash. The twisting road to the ski centre was lined with trees in Christmas card mode, the deciduous ones loaded with snow, the weight bowing the branches in supplication, the denuded ones dotted with teardrops of ice glittering and glistening as they dripped from bare branches.

The true face of the day wasn't revealed until I arrived in the open sweep of the main car park. Here the bitter west wind was driving spindrift across the sparse scattering of cars, their occupants struggling to stand upright long enough to climb into their layers.

I looked up the funicular route which disappeared into a thick bank of cloud keeping the main summit of Cairn Gorm hidden. There were a few hardy souls setting off for the hill, groups of Glenmore Lodge instructors and clients, Arctic-ready, heading for a winter skills session in testing conditions. I decided not to follow suit; the wind was screaming across from the west, and any ascent from here would involve arriving on the summit plateau face first into the teeth of the gale. I got back in the car and drove a short distance back down the road to the empty Sugar Bowl car park.

I was enacting Plan B, taking the more sheltered way in to the Northern Corries then figuring it out from there. It would mean a little extra distance but aesthetically it was a superior start to the walk with the path slipping down through the trees to Utsi's Bridge and then up on to the path towards the Chalamain Gap. This also provided a sweeping view of the Northern Corries, their grandeur stretched over the horizon.

The deep, snow-clad heather was a constant drag but patches of blue sky up front kept the head up and I was making decent time, so much so that I was able to divert into the mouth of the massive Coire an Lochan. I considered the prospects of taking a rising traverse to the right to try to reach the plateau and a westerly march around the corniced rims to Cairn Gorm but there was also doubt in my mind about this being the best way to go.

No, I had come here to visit the corrie of the snows, to at least fulfil one of the connections on this moon walk. And although the weather had given me a few hours' grace, the forecast suggested it was scheduled to deteriorate fast. The likelihood of topping out on Cairn Gorm was slim, the chances of witnessing the full moon up there even slimmer, so although I still held on to the prospect of climbing up on to the Fiacaill a' Choire Chais ridge, I was determined to get my consolation in the bag.

I came round the shoulder of the lower part of the Fiacaill Ridge and picked up the path into Coire an t-Sneachda. As I headed in on the iced path, crampons now attached, there was a steady stream of people heading the other way, some wearing goggles to combat the direct drive of the wind, some without, eyes streaming, red with the force of the unfaltering gusts.

I reached the boulder field under the surrounding soaring sheets of rock with the light fading. Cloud was piling in and there was a thunderous moaning from the wind sweeping across the top of the cliffs, the sound of a massive, all-consuming beast bearing down. The sound was frightening yet awe-inspiring. I stood rooted to the spot like a potential victim in an old horror film, unable or unwilling to tear my eyes away, to flee this oncoming threat, instead frozen in fascination at the power of this as yet invisible maelstrom hurtling towards me.

I finally managed to emerge from this temporary trance, turned and looked south. The skyline was a tenebrous, fast-moving mass, filling every centimetre of the horizon, sucking away every last vestige of light.

Strange what goes through the mind at times like this. There was an inner calm, an admiration of the savage beauty unfolding in front of my eyes. The colour scheme was tipping from dark grey to black, flipping through every subtle tint on the spectrum. For a brief moment, I saw a shade I had been searching out for years, too dark for grey, too light for black. I had long been hoping to find a shirt that colour; typical that nature had finally found for me that perfect tone that had proved impossible even in paint charts, and equally typical that there was no way of capturing a swatch for comparison.

§

The snow started driving across the corrie with excessive force, the wind baring its teeth and screaming like a banshee. The darkness became more absolute and everything disappeared into a confusion of monochrome, every shade merging and swirling round like a cartoon Tasmanian Devil on speed, blinding in its ability to wipe out the landscape.

Any attempt to go higher would have been foolhardy. There was no chance of seeing the moon, only the prospect of battling ferocious white-out conditions in the teeth of that howling gale, so I retreated.

High winds are the most unpleasant and unsettling mountain conditions and gauging just where the limits of your comfort zone are can be difficult. When accompanied by heavy snow or rain they can suck the energy out of you at an alarming rate. Mobility can quickly become affected and progress difficult, even impossible. It becomes difficult to stick to any kind of consistent course. Straying off course, even by only a metre or two, can lead on to dangerous ground.

High winds are a regular feature of life in the Cairngorms. The country's strongest ever gust of 173mph was recorded on Cairn Gorm on March 20, 1986, but even that is thought to have been surpassed. In December, 2008, an anemometer near the summit registered a gust of 194mph but as there was no official recording it could not be verified.

Wind forecasts are based on the Beaufort Scale, rated from 0 to 12. It's a system originally designed for maritime conditions back in the 1800s which has been adapted and adjusted over the years to become the main source of comparison for wind speeds.

0 – Calm air (0-1mph): Water like glass, smoke rises straight. A rare event in Scotland, as likely as spotting a yeti.

1 – Light air (2-3): Ripples on the water, smoke drifts in wind direction. No real effect on walking but you may become irritated by anyone in your party having a sneaky fag.

2 – Light breeze (4-7): Rustling leaves, swaying grass, small wavelets on water. You feel the wind on your face.

3 – Gentle breeze (8-12): Leaves and twigs move, whitecaps on water, hair ruffled, loose clothing flaps. Temporary blindness can be caused by untethered straps

whipping up to smack you in the eye.

4 – Moderate Breeze (13-18): Tree branches sway, small dust devils form, there are small waves and whitecaps and your nice new hairstyle is disarranged. Baldies strut around looking smug.

5 – Fresh Breeze (19-24): Small trees sway, walking takes more effort. Windy Wilson starts getting interested.

6 – Strong Breeze (25-31): Large trees move, whistling can be heard through the foliage, spray blows off water, steady walking becomes difficult.

7 – Near gale (32-38): Trees bend and sway en masse, constant buffeting, rucksack covers, map cases and loose items of clothing can suddenly disappear.

8 – Gale (39-46): Branches snap off trees, walking extremely difficult, even dangerous. Ferries disrupted, bridges closed to high vehicles.

9 – Strong gale (47-54): Whole trees sway, debris blown around, heavy spray on water, walking – and talking – near impossible. Even crawling is difficult. Time to retreat.

10 – Storm (55-63): Trees torn up, widespread damage, progress impossible even by crawling. Not conditions for a stroll unless you are from the Outer Hebrides.

11 – Violent Storm (64-71): Trees uprooted, severe damage, mountainous waves. You would have to be slightly unhinged to consider going out in this.

12 –Hurricane (72+): Batten down the hatches. High probability of serious damage to landscape and buildings.

The wind I was walking in now would probably register as a six or seven, but with the driven snow and the angle of its attack it was hard to be sure. I had certainly been out in far worse wind conditions, but never alone and never in the dark.

The worst I had ever encountered was on Cruach Ardrain

back in 1993 when it took exceptional conditions to prevent us getting our Munro ticks. We had struggled on along the ridge despite the unrelenting battering we were taking but it was a losing battle and now we were on our knees. Standing up was difficult, walking near impossible, so we crawled to the shelter of some rocks to regroup. Then we saw the dog flying.

Scoop, our faithful four-legged mountain companion in the early years, had been caught by one gust and lifted a few feet to the left. He managed to make it over to us, whimpering and whining. That made up our minds – we were getting off the hill. High winds had been forecast but this was far, far worse than predicted. The wind was channelling its force straight at us. It had been building in strength from the start of the walk, and by the time we were high on the wide ridge it had reached a screaming crescendo.

At first, we were convinced this was just a blip and it would soon ease. It got worse. And by the time the dog had turned into a kite, the only option was to abandon our ambitions and get to safety.

Just a couple of years ago, three of us fought our way up the north ridge of Beinn Teallach using the rocks as relief from ferocious gusts which knocked us sideways, but we never doubted we would make it to the summit. The only casualty that day was my rucksack cover which was torn away, last seen heading for Fort William at high speed. I can always picture some poor sod out shopping when suddenly a sheet of grey canvas descends to wrap itself around his or her head.

§

THE ground I had walked in on was now unrecognisable, the path nowhere to be seen. In typical Cairngorms style, it had taken only seconds to turn this into a different landscape, a great unknown.

I stuck religiously to my compass line, ignoring any temptation to try to find the path. This would only waste precious seconds. The important thing now was to drop height and get as far out of this mayhem as possible. This took me on to mixed ground, sheets of angled, solid snow one moment, deep heather with hidden boulders the next. This kind of walking plays havoc with cramponed feet. It precipitates a stumbling, awkward gait, an inability to form any kind of uniform step. One minute they are a godsend, the next a liability. There was no right and there was no wrong. They were slowing me down and causing me to stumble, and yet it would have been unwise to have taken them off, especially with the darkness hiding so many potential traps.

Still the snow was piling in horizontally from my left, restricting my visibility to the few steps ahead and to the right. The eyelashes on my left eye were starting to freeze shut, the wind forcing me to look right most of the time.

Despite the dark, there was an eerie whiteness, a dancing maelstrom of tiny particles which teased and tested, promising a view that never materialised. In Iceland, this is referred to as the white darkness. It perfectly described the landscape I was now in.

At one point, two larger white bullets shot across my eyeline in the gloom, ptarmigan startled by my presence and heading for another bolthole, radar perfectly attuned to find their sanctuary in this turmoil of white. I envied them their confidence and natural instinct. I would have to rely on the compass, and my bolthole was still a long way off.

There never seemed to be any downhill but I was happy to stay with a higher line, the feeling that I would soon be on safer ground. Dropping too soon could lead into more strength-sapping terrain. Walking blindly always seems to make time drag. I felt I had been going for hours: in reality it was just over an hour. But just when I felt that I was getting nowhere, I spotted a dim orange light way off in the distance: I was nearing the ski centre. It's hardly a thing of beauty, but I have to admit a little relief at its presence. There were a few vehicles around, mostly snow machines, but otherwise little sign of life.

It was only a short walk down to my car from here, but it was at this moment I was given another reminder into the importance of keeping your gear in top condition. As I set off for the descent on the ski road, my head torch went out. I always carry a spare, but it made me consider again what a disaster it would have been to lose your one source of light in these conditions.

The practical problems would be bad enough but there could also have a massive psychological effect, a feeling of helplessness that could induce panic and lead to wrong decision making. The problem, as it turned out, was minor, some water ingress which just needed a wipe clear, but the intricacies of trying to do this on a dark hillside with the winds whipping across your hands and body are troublesome. There's also the perils of having to take off heavy winter gloves to fiddle with the delicate battery cover and the potential for one of the gloves to be swept off into the night. The ideal solution is to have a second torch, fully charged and ready to go, which can be swapped with the minimum of fuss.

In the heyday of my night walking I used a head torch only sparingly, relying instead on my night vision to kick in fast. The torch was always there in my rucksack, with spare bulbs and batteries packed separately, but I preferred to try to do without it as much as possible.

Most of the time that was fine. Apart from the night I

walked smack into a tree, of course. That was the exception rather than the rule. I had the eyes of a cat – think I will go private for my next operation – and the more my night vision remained unspoiled by artificial light, the better. I doubt I could do it now. Age takes its toll on all the senses, and eyesight is no different. I can no longer head off from the car without a light shining the way.

I carried out an experiment during a night descent of Beinn Eighe a few years ago. It had been a calm day and the path is well-engineered and obvious, but at one point I switched off my light and stood still. Suddenly I was blind. Now that may sound rather like a contender for Basil Fawlty's suggested *Mastermind* subject for Sybil, The Bleedin' Obvious, but when you are walking along with a light shining the way you can forget just how absolute the darkness can be in a deep corrie or in the shadow of a towering mountain slope.

There have been a couple of occasions since which made me realise just how helpless I would be without a head torch, once in a wood under Lochnagar, the other while going through the Chalamain Gap.

A head torch is a necessity but it's just as important to make sure it is in good working order. Even if you have no cause to use it, you must make sure it is primed for action. Hauling it out from the bottom of your bag only to discover it's not working would be a disaster. I test my torches before every outing. They may have been working last week – check they are still working. If I am heading for a longer walk that I reckon may entail walking in the dark, I put in fresh batteries before I set off.

Make sure you are familiar with all the fittings and know how to open and close it. Speed and familiarity could save vital seconds in an emergency. Sitting on a pitch-dark hillside in a howling gale trying to read the instructions is not a good idea. Besides, you would need a torch to read them. Take spare batteries and, if you have an older torch, a spare bulb. Keep them tightly sealed and easy to access in a different part of your bag.

During the winter months, I always carry at least two torches. On this occasion, however, I didn't have time to activate my spare torch. As I searched my bag in the darkness, my back turned to the driving wind and snow, a police patrol car drove into the car park, circling and checking for waifs and strays and possible stranded motorists.

"Are you alright, sir?"

I wasn't 100 per cent sure if they were talking in the moment or if it was a more long-term existential query. The answer to the first was simple, the second would take a bit longer and quite a few therapy sessions.

I decided that option one was probably the right one and replied that I was, indeed, all right, and that I was just heading down to my collect my car. There was no need to think twice about the next question:

"Would you like a lift?"

This was policing at its finest, a true public service, caring and considerate. I climbed into the back, crampons still fitted to the boots and snow dripping all over the place with the instant warmth of the interior. They even stayed to see if my car – now buried under a blanket of snow and the only one in the car park – would start.

I hadn't seen the Blue Moon on the blue mountain but I had at least been helped out by the boys in blue. Luckily, I hadn't partaken of the Blue Moon beer. A breathalyser test at this juncture may not have been ideal.

The roads were somewhat trickier on the way out but once back on the main road there was no problem. Then it happened, just as I suspected it would. Just 20 miles or so down the A9 the Blue Moon appeared in all its glory. All that time and effort to no avail and now it shows its face. It didn't help that right on cue, The Who came on the radio singing I Can See For Miles. It just reinforces my contention that somewhere in the heavens there's a Department of Irony, and it takes its duties very seriously.

I felt like the person organising a party and passing out the invitations, only for the star attraction to say they couldn't make it. Then you are pass another house and spot your would-be guest of honour living it large with someone else.

This celestial cylinder of angst disappeared after a few minutes as if ashamed of being a spoilsport, but re-appeared further down the road near Pitlochry reinvigorated. Right above Ben Vrackie as it happened, clear as a bell. I knew I should have gone there.

I consoled myself with the thought that this project is not just about full moons, but rather about the challenges of the mountains and the weather. It also cemented the fact that I should try to give myself a little more flexibility in some of my future choices instead of sticking rigidly to set targets.

3
No Wriggle Room

WORM MOON

(Friday, March 2, 00.51)
Mountain*: Beinn a' Bheithir*
Soundtrack*: Dark Side of the Moon – Pink Floyd*
Non-celebratory drink*: Cobra*

I had always reckoned the third full moon of the year, the Worm Moon, would turn out to be the problem child of the 13. Unfortunately, I was to be proved right.

Early March, the first full moon of the meteorological spring, when the earthworms begin to wriggle their way upwards and the birds take full advantage of this smorgasbord of invertebrates. But despite their crucial contribution to the circle of life, it seems worms have been completely ignored when it comes to naming conventions. Sgurr na Boiteag would be a lovely name for a mountain but there doesn't seem to be one anywhere.

Finding a mountain link to the likes of a Blue Moon or a Wolf Moon was simple, but a Worm Moon? This would require some alternative thinking. I looked at going down the serpent route; snakes, dragons and other mythical beasties that are said to lurk in our lochs. This land is awash with legends and creepy-crawlies are no exception.

There's Carn na Nathrach, the 'cairn of the adders', a Corbett in the heart of Ardgour, but despite being a lovely hill in a lovely setting it still lacked the extra wow factor that might have persuaded me make an exception to my Munro-only rule. I would also be heavily reliant on a ferry crossing and a winding B-road over a high pass which had proved problematic before in winter months.

Beinn a' Bheithir, that beautifully twin-peaked mountain at Ballachulish, its deep V splitting the Munros of Sgorr Dhonuill and Sgorr Dhearg was the strongest contender. It has links to a monstrous serpent which was notorious for devouring unwary travellers, until it was despatched by Charles the Skipper. The sea captain lured it out to his ship with a feast, but to reach the food the beast had to cross a causeway made from wooden barrels covered with poisonous stakes and it was fatally impaled.

This mountain never fails to thrill. The sweep of the ridge to Sgorr Dhearg from its attendant top, Sgorr Bhan, is particularly stunning, an almost flawless curve that seems to separate the landscape equally into snow white and shadow black like a precisely folded sheet of paper.

I checked out mountains with strong bird connections. There's a certain logic for a night walk where the early bird gets the worm (moon). Creag Meagaidh was a contender, a wonderful, sprawling lump of rock with a remarkable success story in regenerated woodland in its lower reaches, rich in bird and insect life. During one walk into the heart of this mountain, I took a ten-minute time-out to watch a bellowing of male bullfinches, swift red flashes all preened and puffed up, ready for the serious business of courting, oblivious to their audience.

Unfortunately, the only beastie I ended up seeing was that one that came roaring in from the east, paralysing much of the country. The snow piled up and the roads became impassable. The natural world seemed to be in suspended animation, a petrified victim of a barometrical Medusa, one look into her eyes enough to cause a standstill. My dilemma over which mountain to pick became an irrelevance. Creag Meagaidh and Beinn a' Bheithir were now well out of reach. I thought that if I could at least make it out past Perth, I could reach the sanctuary of the mountains of the west where conditions were not so severe. The worm link didn't matter any more, neither did the Munro rule. Any decent mountain by moonlight would do. Then came the red alerts.

In the days when I was regularly night walking, it was always the thought of the driving that scuppered the outing rather than hill conditions. It's no fun to spend an anxious three-hour drive, hands gripping the steering wheel tightly to rectify the slightest slide, just for your plans to be thwarted on arrival. Even worse getting stuck on a single-track road and the possibility of having to call for assistance. Sometimes you just have to accept the inevitable. It pained me to sit tight, especially looking at some glorious sunsets way out west, but our mountain rescue teams already had their work cut out helping the emergency services extricate stranded motorists and those in remote areas cut off by the snows. It would be irresponsible to ignore their advice and press on regardless for the sake of a pastime. You would be as popular as a Campbell's soup sales rep in Glen Coe.

Part of the lure of the Scottish mountains in winter is the challenge that different weather conditions can throw up. We have the freedom to rise to these challenges, but with that freedom comes responsibility. One of the essential mountain skills is knowing when to turn back. It's also a great discipline knowing when not to attempt it at all. This was one of those times.

For final confirmation, I asked Siri and was told: "You'd be aff yer heid." Said it all, really.

Among the other links I had explored for this moon was that of the worm as a Shakespearean metaphor for a troubled conscience, and in a similar vein, Edgar Allen Poe's poem, The Conqueror Worm, which paints life as merely 'a mad folly ending in hideous death'. These now seemed to resonate more and more as I weighed up my options for the task in hand.

Apart from the so-called Beast from the East, I was also having to deal with the pest in the chest, a stubborn cold which was taking its time to shift. It was just another addition to a catalogue of nagging doubts which confirmed my no-go.

There certainly wouldn't have been much sign of bird life in the blizzard-blasted tree cover of Creag Meagaidh anyway. The worms would have had to have got hold of mini pneumatic drills to have broken through the frozen surface.

Even a short walk down to the seashore in unceasing snow storms failed to render a glimpse of the Worm Moon. The prospect of a full house was never on the cards. I always knew I would lose one or two along the way, and that I would have to make last-minute changes to the schedule. The manner of this defeat was the problem. I had miscalculated, and now I felt trapped, increasingly frustrated as the days and hours ticked past, the moon coming and going, my chance wasted. My lid would have to remain screwed on tight to prevent a major blow-out.

§

WINTER may have arrived late, but it had smashed its way into the party with a vengeance. We'd had typical freeze/thaw cycles through the early part of February, some beautiful white days contrasted with warmer, more benign conditions at times as the full moon of January 31 was eaten away gradually day by day until there was just blackness.

For the first time since 1999, there was no full moon in February. This phenomena has given rise to the new moon being referred to as a black moon. This is not a well-known astrological term, but it has become more commonly used. There are a few other definitions of what can constitute a black moon. It can be the second new moon in the same month. These are the most common, occurring about once every 29 months. It can also be the third new moon in a season of four. These are rarer, about once every 33 months, the exact opposite of a Blue Moon.

By the time the moon emerged from the darkness and was approaching full strength again, it was ambushed. According to the meteorological calendar, March 1 was the start of spring, but this full moon was now battling full winter conditions. At this rate even the astronomical spring date of March 20 was looking optimistic.

The astronomical seasons refer to the position of Earth's orbit in relation to the sun and take into account the equinoxes and solstices. Meteorological seasons are based on the annual temperature cycle and measure the meteorological state as well as coinciding with our calendar to determine a clear shift between the seasons.

Since the seasons vary in length, the start date can fall on different days each year. This makes it difficult to compare seasons between different years and resulted in the introduction of the meteorological calendar, which splits the seasons into four periods of three months: spring (March, April, May), summer (June, July, August), autumn (September, October, November) and winter (December, January, February). It's easier to compare seasonal and monthly statistics this way, although in Scotland's wild and unpredictable climate, all bets are off.

The astronomical seasons run around three weeks later than those of the meteorological one. The astronomical calendar determines the seasons due to the tilt of the Earth's axis in relation to its orbit around the sun. Solstices and equinoxes are considered to be the transition points between the seasons and mark key stages in the astronomical cycle of the Earth.

There are two equinoxes (spring and autumn) and two solstices (summer and winter). The dates aren't fixed due to the Earth's elliptical orbit of the Sun. In early January the sun is closest to the Earth – this is known as perihelion – and in early July it is most distant – aphelion.

During the equinox, day and night will be around the same length. The spring equinox marks the point where the day starts becoming longer than the night, and the autumn equinox is when the night starts to become longer than the day.

The length of day and night are only almost equal on the equinox. This is because the sun appears as a disc, and the top half rises above the horizon before the centre. Sunlight is also refracted by Earth's atmosphere, and so appears to rise before its centre is at the horizon giving more daylight than you might expect (12 hours 10 minutes on the equinox).

Equilux is the term used to signify when day and night are equal. This happens a few days before the spring equinox and a few days after the autumn one. These occur twice a year and are referred to as solstices. The summer solstice – which occurs around June 21 in the Northern Hemisphere – is the day with the longest light while the winter solstice – on or around December 21 – is the day with the shortest amount of light.

During the summer solstice, areas north of the Arctic circle get sunlight for 24 hours, while areas south of the Antarctic circle have a full day of total darkness. This situation is reversed at the winter solstice. At the summer solstice, the sun reaches its highest point of the year, while at the winter solstice, the noon sun is the lowest it will be all year.

You could have been mistaken for believing we had been relocated to somewhere deep in the Arctic: almost constant darkness, mind-numbing cold and snow piled up at waist, and even head, height. The year so far had lacked any kind of consistency. The weather windows had only been open for relatively short periods. High winds had been the driving force, with sunshine and blue sky days few and far between. But just as February was drawing to a close, the weather system dubbed the Beast from the East arrived. It was all the result of an event known as sudden stratospheric warming over the North Pole. Temperatures there rose 40 degrees over a few days, going from -75 to -35. The Arctic air mass split and blocks of polar air were driven southwards. This reversal of fortune in the polar cycle meant a massive switch to easterly air flows, which drag in our weather from Siberia and Norway. It struck fast and hard, so fast that the Daily Express hardly had time to dig out its annual 'White Hell' headline before we were up to our armpits in the stuff.

Normally when a huge dump of snow arrives, it's a godsend for mountaineers. The chance of having three or four days in a row with favourable weather is a dream scenario. A cold settling of the weather gives the snow the chance to firm up, making for easier movement with crampons rather than the uneven and unpredictable manner of walking through deep, soft drifts one minute and over rock-solid slopes the next. The biting cold is a minor irritation when you can see forever, and these days of near perfection are the ones that stick in the memory.

Just a week earlier, we had been bemoaning the fact that the deep, soft snow and benign conditions we had encountered on the hill had disappeared with a sudden rise in the mercury, giving way to slithering ascents on slush and mud, crampons a dead weight in the rucksack. Now the snow had returned with a vengeance, and this lot looked like it wouldn't be going anywhere soon. Unfortunately, neither did my proposed moon walk on Beinn a Bheithir. I had missed my window of opportunity to get to Glen Coe. It was foolhardy to even attempt the road journey. Every avenue of escape from home was blocked: I was struggling to even get the car out of the drive, and the town was temporarily cut off.

Even if I could have made it to the foot of the mountain, the risk wasn't worth it. The sudden, massive accumulation of snow would have meant struggling through waist-deep drifts in a ghostly landscape with few visible points of reference. The avalanche danger was also at the highest setting, heavily laden slopes and overhangs ready to snap, one short crack the only warning before a wall of white swept everything aside in the blink of the eye. There had already been more avalanches in our mountains than in the previous year, and this constant danger had been hampering mountain rescue search missions for three missing walkers. At times, it is simply too perilous to carry on. Nature will run her course and we are completely insignificant in her grand plan. With all this in mind, I reluctantly decided to sit tight and wave goodbye to the Worm Moon.

§

THE great outdoors is good for the body and the soul. It's also good for the mind. When I was a teenager and first started suffering black moods, I was able to take my frustrations out at the weekend on the football pitch. I often came off second best in the meaty tackles department, but at least the previous week's anxieties had been washed away. I would arrive home limping, shins and ankles ripped and torn, but with a sense of satisfaction that this would carry me through the next seven days. My mum, in the usual supportive manner of a concerned parent, was always horrified.

"You're going to lose a leg at this rate," was her understated reaction.

I'm happy to report that all my limbs are still intact but recurrent knee problems eventually put a premature end to my football days. By this time, I was working in newspapers and the midweek days and weekend started to fuse into one, the working hours longer and more anti-social. It was a boom or bust style of job. The often frenetic pace had the advantage of keeping the mind busy, but there could also be long lulls with not enough to do and too much time to think.

I was fortunate that my black spells were – and still are – short-lived. There seemed no real reason for the descent into those dark spaces, no obvious trigger. It would usually start in the late afternoon or evening and I would just feel myself sinking further and further into the pit. The night would be restless, the sleep, if any, disturbed, and this would carry on into the next day before I would start the gradual climb back out from the depths. During this 24 or 36-hour spell, like many others who suffer similarly, I occasionally pondered taking that final step, but thankfully those ideas never made it off the drawing board. When my job became all-consuming, I decided I needed an outlet, something that could open the pressure valve and let off steam. The hills became my saviour. This was a pastime that could fit round any schedule, that meant I didn't have to depend on anyone else. It became an antidote to the rigours of work and everyday life, and over time, it has become a way of life. There's no down side. Whenever the black dog is waiting at the door for walkies, I pick up the lead and go. I'm usually out around twice a week on average during the year. Sometimes that can be seven days in a row, sometimes just the once in any week. But it's a pastime that continually needs fed. If the period stretches to two weeks without getting out, I can feel the outdoors equivalent of the shakes. My mood changes, the restlessness grows.

I have been lying in bed at night, wide awake, staring at the ceiling, not wanting to turn on the light for the fear of waking my wife, Alison, unaware that she is also awake and aware that I am awake.

When I do finally twig that has she cottoned on, I whisper sweet nothings in her ear:

"I think I'll go out for a walk."

The reply is simply: "Okay."

Year after year of accepting this strange behaviour have conditioned her responses. She knows it is pointless to argue. Some five hours later and I am sitting at the top of Buachaille Etive Mor watching the sun begin its unrelenting march into a new day. Not sleeping is a simple tonic for insomnia.

I didn't have that option when the Beast bared its fangs. I had deliberately kept off the hills for the ten days previously to plan and prepare for the Worm Moon outing, so this was a double whammy. Not only had I had been prevented from my endorphin-fulfilling walk, but this failure threatened to blow a great big hole in my moon walk project. There was pacing, there was fidgeting. There was the inability to focus on any task, or book, or television programme.

I was channelling Marvin the Paranoid Android from The Hitchhikers' Guide to the Galaxy.

"The first 24 hours were the worst, and the second 24 hours were the worst too. The third 24 hours I didn't enjoy at all. After that I went into a bit of a decline."

Rather than being the third tick on the list of 13 full moons, the Worm Moon expedition had turned into a metaphorical game of Dungeons and Dragons, all black moods and recurring dreams of writhing serpents. I had adopted the Homer Simpson pose, lying on the couch watching daytime television. I hadn't quite gone full Jeremy Kyle yet, but Tipping Point's regular viewing figures had definitely been given a boost. The Chinese refer to this moon as the Sleepy Moon. There was plenty of that going on, just at the wrong times of day. Sir Sleepalot was in his prime.

Boredom even drew me to the astrology charts. I knew about the birth signs that were based around the sun which are said to dictate your personality, but hadn't realised there are also moon signs which represent inner emotions. Together they are said to influence your emotional mode of operation. When I pared down through the gobbledygook, I was informed that during this moon Virgo was a huge influence and that I was carrying a sign of good luck. It seemed a bit odd to be relying on a snooker pundit for this information; no wonder it was so wildly out.

It was starting to get to Alison. After one of her suggestions of relaxation was met with a downbeat reply, as she left the room in frustration she said:

"Why don't you go down for a walk along the water."

I'm sure I heard the sentence finish with "... and throw

yourself in" but I wouldn't be able to swear to it in court.

I don't suppose it's surprising that the chosen music for this was Dark Side of the Moon with its themes of vacuous capitalism leading inevitably to an unfulfilled life and the subsequent descent into madness. This was an old favourite; somewhat perversely, considering the themes, it provided a soothing soundtrack on these long night drives in the darkness through lonely glens and soaring mountain silhouettes.

It's a term that has become synonymous with the hidden, or darker, side of humanity, but without wishing to ruin the moment for the 45 million plus who have bought the Pink Floyd album, there is no dark side of the moon. Both sides see the same amount of sunlight, but we only ever see one face. The moon rotates in exactly the same time it takes to orbit the Earth, so the same side is always facing us. The only humans to have seen the other side of the moon are space travellers.

The effects of the moon on the human psyche have long been a fascination, with the belief that a full moon can alter and control behaviour patterns. Ancient philosophers blamed mania on the evil influence of the Roman moon goddess, Luna, hence the origin of the word 'lunatic'. It has been blamed for sleep deprivation, epilectic seizures and animal attacks, and it was also suggested it could enhance fertility. Another belief often mooted was that because the human body is 75 per cent water, and the moon's gravitational pull affects the rise and fall of the tides on Earth, it could have an analogous effect on us.

These beliefs have persisted throughout the centuries, and despite scientific fact debunking every one of them, they remain a frame of reference in modern times, especially when it comes to the darker deeds.

There are studies showing that sleep patterns can be

significantly affected by lunar phases. Participants in one experiment got around 20 minutes less sleep during a full moon, the theory being they were exposed to more light before going to sleep. I have had problems with sleep for nearly 40 years, but I've always put that down to strange work patterns rather than an excess of moonlight. If it comes to a choice, give me the moonlight every time.

Even though I had missed the Worm Moon, I felt I should still raise a glass to its presence as per the programme. I suppose the true disciple would have opted for a bottle of mescal, but didn't feel it was a drink to enjoy at home and I had recently gone on a worm-free diet. Anyway, if I had been prepared to go down the hardcore route, it should have been absinthe, or anything else containing wormwood, but the last thing I needed was more hallucinations.

My mind also flashed back to days working in The Scout Bar in Dundee when a pint of snakebite – a mix of lager and cider, sometimes with a dash of blackcurrant – was all the rage, especially with the female clientele, although I remembered it more from the perspective of the volume of vomit that had to be hosed off the floor most nights. It wasn't a fond memory, and I expect it would likely have brought up more bad ones.

I did look into a Scottish-produced beer called Snake Venom, but it's the world's strongest clocking in at 67.5 per cent ABV and costs around £50 a bottle. That's a lot of money just to bring on a coma for a few days. With a brew this powerful, you might as well just shove a puff adder down your trousers and be done with it.

Mark Twain wrote: "Everyone is a moon, and has a dark side which he never shows to anybody." Any of the options so far would have gone a long way to proving that statement wrong.

In the end, I settled for simplicity and consoled myself with a Cobra and the thought that I would ramp up the preparations for the next walk. I was determined to make sure I wouldn't lose another one.

4

Night Skye

BLUE MOON

(Saturday, March 31, 13.36)
Mountain*: Bla Bheinn (Blaven)*
Soundtrack*: White Room – Cream*
Celebratory drink*: Skye Blaven*

Midnight in Skye. I'm sitting in the car on the shores of tranquil Loch Slapin watching the full moon drifting lazily through patchy sheets of cloud. One minute it's lighting up the dark waters, the next it has dipped behind a curtain of gauze. It's hide and seek on a celestial scale.

I'm resting before starting a night ascent of Bla Bheinn, the blue mountain. This is the fourth full moon walk and all the signs are promising that it will be the best yet.

So much for the saying 'Once in a blue moon': this is the second Blue Moon of the year, a phenomenon that only happens four or five times every century. When there are two in a year, the first Blue Moon always occurs in January, the second predominantly in March. Occasionally it can happen in April and on rare occasions in May or December.

For a Blue Moon to take place in March, there can be no Full Moon in February, so non leap years will inevitably be favoured. We haven't had a double Blue Moon since 1999 and the next won't come round until 2037.

Bla Bheinn was the only real choice. The list had to include at least one Skye Munro, and Bla Bheinn is regarded by many as the finest mountain on the Misty Isle, isolated from the main Black Cuillin ridge. It's a masterpiece of rock sculpture, soaring cliffs, carved faces and an abundance of towers and protuberances bursting on to the ridge lines on the gradually curving approach to the main summit. And once you arrive at the trig pillar which marks the highest point, you are greeted by the unrivalled sight of the Cuillin ridge spilling across the horizon, every individual peak present and correct, each with its unique razor-sharp profile, a reminder of the sheer audacity of this place.

It's a mountain I know well and in many moods. I have been up on typical Skye weather days, swirling, clinging mist accompanied by constant drizzle, that peculiar light rain which seems to have signed an exclusivity deal with Scotland and which gives the impression of being wetter than it can possibly be in reality.

I have traversed the summits in blistering heat, a day which marked the arrival of spring in spectacular fashion with a temperature swing of some 25C from the day before when he had been teetering along the ridges in Glen Shiel on ice-encrusted rocks.

And just two years earlier, a friend and I had set off in rain which was morphing into sleet and then snow with every metre gained, and then into heavier and heavier snowfall. The final crossing of the high corrie bowl was through deep powder to gain a short, slippery scramble over a rocky barrier half-buried by drifts to gain easy passage to the pillar. The view at the summit was fleeting, no time to even snap off one picture. The Cuillin were there for a second and then they weren't, but even a split-second sighting is worth all the effort. I was confident I could handle whatever Bla Bheinn had in store this time.

§

THE remnants of the Beast's fury had lingered for a couple of weeks. The sporting calendar was badly hit, football, rugby, horse racing and many other events put on hold. The roads were still suffering and transport was patchier than usual. Ten days after the abandoned Worm Moon walk, I was in Glenshee. The routes we had originally planned had to be adapted, the laybys inaccessible to the coach because of piled-up snow.

Another week on and another planned outing also went by the wayside. I had been scheduled to do a night walk feature for *The Great Outdoors* with comedian Ed Byrne, a regular contributor to the magazine. Ed was performing in Dundee as part of his Spoiler Alert tour, and we were supposed to meet in his dressing room after the show and head off into the hills. There was a short and fairly vicious reprise of the wild weather, however, and it quickly became obvious that venturing into the mountains in the darkness would be madness. Instead, we did what all good Celts do – we retired to the bar to talk about mountains and agreed to meet another time for a night adventure.

Four days later and I was making an early morning ferry crossing of the Corran narrows in icy sunshine and unblemished blue sky to take in the Druim na Sgriodain circuit. The water was like glass, the only whitecaps those of the mountains of Glen Coe and Lochaber. This was now officially spring no matter which calendar you referenced, and we were only five days away from the clocks changing. My heavy winter gear seemed like overkill on the sunshine walk past the walled burial ground and ancient monuments of the Clan Maclean and then the initial climb on steep grassy slopes, but once sufficient height was gained the chill was evident. I reached the final col through increasingly extensive fields of snow, and stared up the final ridge into the blinding sun. The ground was solid. After one or two tentative steps, I stopped to fit my crampons; the angle of the climb was steep enough to suggest a slip could be serious.

It may have been spring at sea level, but up here it was still winter, and it catches many people by surprise. There's often a reluctance to get out the crampons, a feeling that you may just get by without them. Then it's too late. It's always the smart move to fit them before it becomes a necessity.

They can feel like more of a hindrance at times, because of the inconsistency of snow cover. When you are wading through deep, soft snow, they ball up regularly and have to be consistently kicked clear before you hit more solid patches of ground. But it is just not practical to switch between fitting and removing them every time the conditions merit.

There's always a moment when you feel you may need crampons, when you can't kick a step, when the route ahead looks like trouble. That's the point when there should be no hesitation. They may not be needed for long but why take the risk? We've all heard the horror stories about accidents occurring simply because certain parties delayed their decision: One more step will be okay, then that one step proves disastrous.

The last few years have seen increased use of spikes for the use on lower slopes and approaches. The quality has improved immensely, but I would still advocate having crampons for the higher ground. Snow shoes are also becoming used more widely. Sometimes it feels as though we have been invaded by the Inuit. Every year there's more and more equipment to buy, more to add to the weight of the pack. The ideal scenario would be to have spikes for the approach, crampons for higher, steeper slopes and then snow shoes for the crossing of plateaux under deep snow. Don't forget the survival shelter, avalanche beacon and probing poles. Just remember to pack a pack mule and a spare set of knee-caps.

The crampons made for a speedy ascent in the cool of the shadowed flank and I was soon back in the sunshine, standing at the trig pillar gazing over Loch Linnhe to ranks and ranks of peaks stretching forever, the azure sky decorated with spindly flecks of white cloud reminiscent of an artist's sign-off. The route followed a curving line west to the main summit, Druim na Sgriodain. There was a fence line for guidance, but in some places only the tops of the posts were showing above the sea of white. The final descent involved trying to find the least corniced part of the ridge before dropping gingerly to reach the icicle-lined stream which cascaded over a series of slabs and drops before culminating in the huge waterslide of Tubhailt Mhic 'ic Eoghainn (Maclean's Towel). The evening sky was a pastel extravaganza on the return ferry trip, a spectacle of tranquillity which promised better days and nights to come.

The following evening I was in Aberdeen delivering a talk for the North-east Mountain Trust, the lingering sunset on the drive up the coast road the perfect travelling companion. I awoke next day with a heavy cold approaching, but despite being a gold star pessimist, I managed to shake any feelings of dread about whether this would have any impact on my plans for the looming Blue Moon walk. I put the lurgy down to a form of heat exhaustion, a common, short-lived reaction to the white sun of the last walk, and tried to turn it to my advantage. A few days' rest with no distractions or temptations would allow me to fine tune preparations.

I had learned my lesson from the Worm Moon debacle and aimed to set off for Skye with plenty of time to spare. The moon was timed for 13.36 on the Saturday, but the walk would start just after midnight on the Friday, so as long as I arrived on the island early on the Friday, I would have plenty of time to spare.

There was other business to fit in. Around the beginning of February, I had received a call from a PR company asking if I would be interested in shooting a short film to promote a new pocket camera by Canon. My first reaction was that this was a wind-up, but they had read my first book, *Moonwalker*, and thought a night shoot in the Scottish mountains would be an ideal way to showcase this new compact. they liked the fact I regularly used a compact on my hill treks rather than carrying heavier and more technical gear. It would be filmed as a short story: the journey to the hills, the ascent in the dark, the sunrise from the summit, and then a final scene at home with my granddaughter looking back over the pictures of the adventure.

Biggest problem was the timing. They were looking for dates in March, but they also needed weather neutral scenery. Snowscapes were out. They were out of luck at this time of year in Scotland.

We agreed to hold off the filming schedule until May, and I suggested a few landscapes. The likes of Skye and Torridon were appealing but on reflection it was felt they were just too far away for a full crew coming up from the south of England for a few days. The Cairngorms were also considered, but there's always the prospect of snow still smothering the tops here in May. We settled for Glen Coe and Lochaber, and now it was time to act as tour guide for their scouting party.

They had timed the visit to perfection, wall to wall sunshine, frosted grasses and trees sparkling, flocculent belts of cloud lying motionless across the midriffs of distant mountains. The first stop was at picture perfect Lochan na h-Achlaise, then a brief halt at Buachaille Etive Mor to take some photos at the bridge and the ice pancakes in the river, before heading round to Bidean nam Bian and the Three Sisters. The story of the Lost Valley had piqued their interest, but the path up the side of the gorge was coated in thin ice and it would have been foolish to carry on much further. We drove round to Glencoe village and then walked across the lower reaches of Sgurr na Ciche. I could see that this little peak, known as the Pap of Glencoe, had suddenly become a front-runner for the film; it looked far more achievable for a top-heavy camera team unused to mountains, certainly not as intimidating as the giants further up the glen.

We parted company after a refreshment at the Clachaig, they were heading back to Glasgow for a flight south, while I drove on to Invergarry where I would spend the night, ready for an early rousing for my Skye expedition.

§

THE next morning would again be spent scouting, this time in anticipation of the Blue Moon walk. I had plenty of time to kill so the day would a leisurely spell of time management with low-level walks in the sunshine. The first walk had a dual purpose, a visit to Loch Scavaig and the bothy of New Camasunary from the Elgol road that would also provide some further clues as to likely conditions on Bla Bheinn. Winter hadn't quite thrown off its shackles and there were still warnings about solid fields of snow and ice in the higher reaches. I had picked up some of the chatter on social media over the past few days, and there didn't seem anything to get worked up about. It would be a winter ascent with all the care that involves but nothing out of the ordinary.

The frontal view of the blue mountain was showing anything but blue on first viewing. Bla Bheinn sat black and bold above the stripped birches and russet grasses in the morning sunshine, some sign of white patches higher on the slopes. Further round, the long south ridge was clear, a possible alternative for the ascent. It's reckoned to be the surest route in winter conditions.

The car park at the start of the walk-in to the bothy was busy, yet with the biting wind making a mockery of blue skies and bright light, the feeling of isolation was acute. Camasunary is a wonderful spot. There's that grand reveal when you breach the crest of the track and the view to the bay and beach below opens out. It's a Caribbean setting with a Scottish twist. The sun was sparkling on the water, Rum and Eigg just dark silhouettes on the distant horizon. It's hard to think of a more idyllic setting.

But all is not as it seems from distance. Closer examination reveals a beach strewn with jetsam and flotsam, the modern curse of plastic littering the shore. The old bothy hasn't fared too well either. Sitting abandoned at the north end of the bay, its porch has become a dumping ground for campers and walkers, bags of rubbish piled up, a convenience for those unwilling to carry their responsibilities away. It makes the heart sink. Here we have a natural beauty spot, one of which we should be rightly be proud, and yet it is slowly but surely being overwhelmed by the selfishness of a new breed of unthinking outdoor visitor. It's an awkward spot for clean-up squads to visit and there's only so much that can be carried out at any one time. Hats off to the volunteers who have been making such a big effort to turn the tide but you can't help feeling this is akin to painting the Forth Rail Bridge, doomed to be a forever war.

Over the past few years, we have seen a massive surge in Scottish pride at our landscape and culture. Unfortunately, there doesn't seem to have been any great correlation in litter awareness. Littering is a major headache all over the country.

Accidents do happen. Maps, paper tissues, food wrappers and the like are often torn from your hands by the wind, and plastic bottles can fall from rucksack pockets. But I come across too many of them on hill paths for it all to be accidental. Crushed cans? Do me a favour. It's a symptom of the way too many lead their lives.

Ignorance is often cited as a reason for this anti-social behaviour, certain day trippers or casual walkers who only come out when the sun shines, but that's not whole story. A lot of these blots on our landscape are being created by supposedly caring walkers and climbers. How else to explain the orange peel lying scattered amongst the rocks in the higher reaches of the Lota Corrie on Skye? This is the realm of the mountaineer not the casual tourist.

Some of this may be down to a mistaken belief that the likes of orange peel and banana skins biodegrade quickly. They don't. It takes around two years for them to disappear. Cigarette ends are worse, taking up to ten years to vanish. Meanwhile, the discarding of paper tissues is reaching epidemic proportions. I stopped using cotton handkerchiefs in favour of tissues many years ago. A few days on the hill in soggy conditions, and I quickly realised the cotton option was a better bet in my pocket than a pile of mush which tended to disintegrate and blow away in pieces over the day.

And what is with wet wipes – have we all become so

paranoid about even the most minuscule contact with our surroundings? As with tissues, there seems to be a belief that wet wipes will quickly disintegrate. It can take months, and in the meantime they will just keep piling up, a constantly expanding eyesore lying on our paths, among the grass and flowers, floating down streams, hanging from trees.

I have noticed an increase in the number of walkers picking up the discarded waste of others during their trek. It doesn't mean you have to spend the day litter picking, just gather up the odd piece of rubbish you come across. Since the carrier bag charge was introduced, virtually everyone in the country has at least one bag with them at any time. Most walkers have a few in their rucksack, either for their lunch, protection for gear during wet conditions and even for that old trick of sliding on waterproofs fast and easily. It doesn't take much to pick up the odd bit of garbage.

I always carry a spare plastic bag in my rucksack and pick up what I can, but there is only so much you can take if you are out on a day hike. I also draw the line at picking up human waste. If you are unlucky, you may find some used toilet paper lying around. If you are lucky, you may avoid stepping in whatever the paper was used to remove.

Some recent highlights include a drystone wall with several banana skins jammed into the cracks, a pair of underpants left dangling on a fence, and an erect tent dumped off the South Shiel Ridge after the final peak. Who goes to the effort of climbing seven Munros and then discards their tent rather than taking it down with them? Sometimes, the mind really does boggle.

I have reached summits to find someone had tidied up their mess, put it in a bag, then left it wedged into the cairn. It's a common problem in bothies, sacks filled with empty cans, bottles, even clothes, left hanging like a fetid Christmas stocking waiting for some rubbish collecting anti-Santa to take it away. The volunteers who have to trail in for miles and then remove or dispose of your rubbish must think you are wonderful. Get real. There's no bin lorry coming round once a week.

Every piece of discarded clothing, every piece of paper, every tin and bottle, every rancid portion of food waste, is down to the individual. It's simple. If you carry it in, you carry it out. You don't leave it for someone else to deal with. Why would anyone think this is acceptable? If we are truly caring about the environment, we all need to start playing our part.

§

THE recce complete, I headed back over the pass. Then a distant throbbing, and the helicopter came into sight, circling the heights of Bla Bheinn, fading away as it did its circuit, the thunder building again as it continued the loop, over and over on repeat. It's always a sobering sound, a reminder that things can go wrong in the mountains. Here we had the false premise of spring, with winter still waiting in ambush for the unwary and unprepared. It may have been sunshine and blue skies down here, but higher on the ridges and peaks the remaining snow patches can be treacherous. Those heading up believing the days of crampons and axes were over for another year can easily be caught out.

My hopes that this was merely a training exercise for the crew faded somewhat on the return drive. Sitting on the road at the foot of Bla Bheinn was a police rescue vehicle, its occupants no doubt somewhere on the mountain. The good news was that there was no further news that night. Whatever had happened had been resolved without tragedy.

I continued on to part two of the day's leisure activities, driving up the east side of the island, through Portree and past the rocky playgrounds of The Storr and then The Quiraing to reach Trotternish in the north of the island on roads pot-holed and scarred by the ravages of this enduring winter. At one point a section of the surface had risen like a wave requiring motoring skills more akin to surfing, the car looking in danger of rolling on to its side.

The wind had picked up and was whistling along the coast as I took the path out to the bothy known as The Lookout, a former coastguard watch station which sits near the cliff top above Rubha Hunish. The going was soft underfoot but the strong drying wind meant it was never too boggy. Shafts of late sunlight were lasering through the evening skies spilling ever enlarging silver pennies over the water.

I found the bothy occupied, a father and his two excited young sons on a family adventure, sleeping bags laid out on the small platforms, a rough and ready sanctuary at the edge of the island. They were tucking in to an evening meal, the boys enjoying slices of pizza while excitedly giving this stranger the third degree.

"Do you have a tent?"

"Did you come in by boat?"

"Have you considered switching energy suppliers?"

Being cross-examined by youngsters is always a delight, a forthright mixture of excitement and innocence that often proves more revealing to both sides than the most challenging questioning of political correspondents. I even managed to squeeze in a few of my own.

They were from Edinburgh, the boys' east coast twang duelling with dad's Catalan-accented English. I envied them their night adventure, but I had one of my own to make so I said my goodbyes. On the way back to the car, I met a young couple heading in with full packs. It seemed the young practitioners for the Spanish Inquisition would have another couple of victims.

I headed back down the coast and made it to the Sligachan before darkness caught up to grab some refreshment. The pub was heaving, but I was happy to be alone, a silent watcher in a crowd, enjoying the company of the many without the need to be part of the throng. I like being among people, I'm just not so keen to be with them. There's something enormously relaxing about sitting anonymously in the midst of a cosy, crowded pub, the white noise of satisfied chatter swirling round. I was tempted to hang about to join in the pub quiz but decided it was time to get far from the madding crowd and head for the hills.

A short stop for last-minute supplies at the Co-op in Broadford took longer than anticipated thanks to the coffee machine exploding in front of the customer ahead of me, delaying my mocha send-off further. I emerged at last to see the moon looking huge and clear, a brilliance I was relying on for a special ascent. At one point, it really did look blue.

It accompanied me all the way on my second drive of the day round to Loch Slapin, all dark shapes and silent running. I parked across the water from Bla Bheinn, all the better for a full view of the mountain. I managed to rest but sleep was impossible, a constant eye open for my celestial companion's moods.

Every so often, a pair of lights would pierce the darkness miles off down either direction on the road, moving steadily along before being cloaked by the night. Sometimes they would pull off the road and settle down for the night, fellow travellers searching for their own space, with their own agenda of an early start next day or just a quiet time under the stars.

A few hours later, I started up the engine and drove the

short distance round to the mountain car park. There were a few other vehicles scattered around, all in darkness, all silent. The moon had gone AWOL, the cloud had taken over and the top of the mountain was hidden, but I assumed this was temporary, a rest period before the rising of the day.

By 2am I was heading through the trees by torchlight, wrapped in five top layers, snow trousers on, ice axe and crampons at the ready. Despite the chilly breeze, it didn't take too long to overheat. The heavy sigh of the wind sweeping across the grasses was fighting against the rush of the stream deep below in the gorge. The pace along the path was slow and steady, the weight of my clothing and pack a major decider.

An hour later I took a seat by the stream at the mouth of dark Coire Uaigneich watching the moon spotlighting the high col. This was the first feeding stop of the walk, a necessity when breakfast is thrown so out of kilter. The sounds of the wind and water were still with me, yet I felt I was surrounded by silence, one of the great joys of walking alone at night in the mountains.

The moon was dancing in and out of the shifting cloud as I pushed up into the corrie, the shadows and shapes of the faces all around the only clue as to the height gains I was making. It was still with me as I made my way up the clinking confusion of the scree path, occasionally throwing off the dancing veils of wispy cloud to light the way ahead. So far, so good.

At times I had to stop and search ahead for the track of the path with my light as it took an unexpected twist or turn, invisible behind the vast curtain of grey. I squeezed up a rising ramp filled with snow to emerge on a flatter section perched above a deep cut in the mountain. Now the huge gashes in the ridge were markers for my progress.

So far I had only encountered the odd patch of snow, but after I had passed the prominent connecting point near Clach Glas, I hit the first of the serious cover. Here the snow was like rock, rigid and unforgiving. I couldn't manage to kick a step. It would be crampons from here to the top.

I stuck to the right using the deep gashes on the ridge as a handrail, the Great Prow just ahead. Seconds after the angle of the route had started to swing left, I became engulfed in a realm of confusion. I had stepped into a white room – four white walls, a white ceiling and a white floor.

The mist was impenetrable, the line of sight in every direction gone. The cold became more pronounced, the angle of ascent suddenly much more serious. At one point, I seemed to be rising vertically. The snow underfoot was as solid and uncompromising as iron.

I could see nothing ahead, nothing behind. I knew there were huge drops on my right but I couldn't see them. I had been on Bla Bheinn half a dozen times, including in blizzard conditions, yet now I didn't recognise any of it. I could have been anywhere. I picked up a rock to see how far it would roll before stopping. Instead, it bounced like a basketball, gaining height with every bounce, before disappearing into the void.

My watch had abandoned the cause, just a blank screen, overwhelmed by the cold. My phone battery sank into the red then died, another victim of the cold wind. I plugged it into my power pack and buried it in the depths of my rucksack in the hope it would recover for later use. Even the camera was flashing red, useless. I was on my own. I have never felt so intimidated on a mountain.

I continued cautiously, making sure every step was firmly planted. I figured so long as I kept rising on the angle, I would be okay. It wasn't a pleasant experience. When I finally reached the trig pillar, I felt like kissing it. Except my lips would probably have become welded to the stone. Explain that one to mountain rescue.

It was too cold to hang around, and there was no chance of a moon view or a sunrise. I front pointed my way down at times, a mental security blanket. When I finally came out of the snowline, the relief was such that I felt my legs were going to give way. The morning colours were muted, the distant sunrise a brief flash, the mountain behind me still buried in cloud.

I heard a bleep from inside my bag and stopped to take the phone. It had come back to life now that I descended from the dead zone. I switched it on and was greeted by a confusion on screen. Everything flashed up confused, the letters and numbers appearing as something resembling Cyrillic for a few seconds before normal service resumed. I checked to see that I hadn't lost track of time in the icy mist only to emerge 24 hours later on April Fool's Day. Perhaps I had just caught the tail end of a mass phone hack by Putin and Co. It was a bizarre end to a strange night.

The walk hadn't worked out like I planned but the mountains provide a constant learning curve and I had certainly learned another valuable lesson. I thought I knew Bla Bheinn like the back of my hand but I had been shown that you can become disoriented anywhere. These are wild places and there is no room for error or over-confidence. I had a real spring in my step on the way out. It hadn't been the night I had hoped for, but it still felt like a huge victory.

5
Shadows and Afterglow

PINK MOON

(Monday, April 30, 01.58)
Mountain*: Beinn Eighe: Ruadh-stac Mor,*
Spidean Coire nan Clach
Soundtrack*: Moonshadow – Cat Stevens*
Celebratory drink*: Gordon's Pink Gin*

Four full moons down, and hardly a stellar success so far. Three had proved less than ideal in testing winter conditions, while the other hadn't even got out of the starting blocks. I reckoned I was due a break. I also reckoned that if this fifth attempt were to fail then I should just cut my losses and abandon the project. The choice of mountain would be crucial. I needed a spectacular outing to lift the spirits and breathe new life into the mission.

The Pink Moon was named for the wildflowers which started appearing in abundance at this time of year. I could only find two mountains with connections to pink flowers. There was lonely Sgurr na Feartaig, the highest point of a long, curving, multi-topped ridge to the north-west of Loch

Monar. Its name means 'peak of the sea pink', a plant also known as thrift, which is found growing on its slopes, but unfortunately for my purposes it failed to reach the magic 3000-ft mark.

The prevalence of these flowers in this part of the country is highlighted by the fact that not a million miles away, on the eastern side of Loch Monar, lies the almost identically named Sgurr na Fearstaig. It is the western summit on the Strathfarrar ridge, and is a Munro Top of Sgurr Fuar-thuill. Logistics ruled this out; it would mean taking in the full ridge of six peaks, not a problem in itself, but vehicle access to Glen Strathfarrar is restricted to daylight hours, and cars are not allowed to stay in overnight. There is no restriction on cycling or walking up the glen, but the thought of adding this on to an already taxing walk was not realistic.

I then recalled one of the highlights of my mountain days, an impromtu ascent of Beinn Eighe in Torridon in December to catch the dying embers of the day. I climbed up through the spectacular Coire Mhic Fhearchair and on to the summit of Ruadh-stac Mor, before dropping again to hunker down on the slabs beside the stream which tumbles over the lip of the corrie while I waited for nature to do her thing.

The rock walls had already taken on a warm, pinkish hue as the sunshine faded and then sank into the golden hour. The sky turned yellow, then pink, then various tones of purple before deciding to go for it with streaks of every colour. The Flowerdale peaks were just silhouettes amid a riot of colour, the lochan-studded landscape now a purple rash. But it was the red rocks that had lodged firmly in my mind.

There are many mountains named for the reds evident on their slopes and ridges – Scotland is certainly not short on Deargs – but there was only one winner. Beinn Eighe would be my Pink Moon mountain.

The other major selling point was that I would be based just a stone's throw away, and it was also likely that for the first time I would have company. This moon coincided with an annual trip away with mountain friends. Every year around this time, we book a house for a week-long get-together, and this time we had chosen Gairloch. I had a good feeling about this walk – the planets seemed to be in alignment at long last.

§

EASTER had come and gone but the temperature took its time remembering that it was spring. A chocolate egg hunt in Glen Doll with the granddaughters was accomplished only by wearing winter woollies, and an afternoon stroll in the Sidlaws still picked up a crunch underfoot on waterlogged paths.

When the ground had thawed, I was heading far up to the north-east coast for some unfinished business. The last time I had attempted to climb the Morven circuit, I had just locked the car and slung on my rucksack when a jeep-load of tweed-clad chaps pulled up alongside. They told me they were about to do a deer count on the estate, and asked if I would mind postponing my walk for a couple of hours. They were terribly polite, but there was no doubting they expected me to acquiesce. I would have been quite within my rights to refuse, but the last thing you want when setting off on a walk is to have any rancour with the locals. I agreed but I knew that delaying the walk by two hours would mean I couldn't complete the whole circuit in the time I had. I also knew that they knew I would realise this and hope that I would just head off.

Call me childish if you like, but I reckoned I had to get some satisfaction from a ruined day. I told them I would just hang around in the car and read until they were finished. You could tell it wasn't the answer they had expected or wanted. They drove off silently. And politely, of course. My little victory secured, I gave it five minutes then left for more hospitable climes.

It's around six hours to the start of the Morven walk, so I broke the journey by meeting my friend Andy in Ardgay near Bonar Bridge and we made the short yomp up Carn Salachaidh from the parking spot by the old red postbox, which is still attributed to George VI. We hadn't quite got the hang of this spring thing yet so were overheated by the time we came down the hill. We made up for it by having an ice cream in the local coffee shop before we parted company.

I headed on to the Sleeperzzz hostel at Rogart rail station where I spent the night in one of the static railway carriages. I figured I might need more than three z's but there was no extra charge. It's been an old favourite over the years, a handy jumping off point for the Sutherland and Caithness hills. A fast DIY breakfast in the dining car, a scraping of ice from the car windows, and I was driving north up the near-empty A9. The sun rose with such nuclear brightness it made the landscape darker, sunglasses a must to avoid driving into a ditch.

I passed Golspie and the statue of the dastardly Duke of Sutherland on Ben Bhraggie without lowering myself to making any rude gestures in his direction. I passed Brora, then Helmsdale, created in 1814 as a fishing village by ruthless landowners to 'persuade' those crofters forced off the surrounding lands to try the sea for a living. When I finally reached my starting point at Braemore along the twisting single-track road from Dunbeath, I'm happy to report there was no sign of a deerstalker or a pair of tweed trews anywhere. There was, however, a cacophony of birdsong puncturing the otherwise silent landscape. This is the Flow Country, the largest area of blanket bog in Europe, stretching some 4,000 square kilometres. Those who walk regularly in Scotland are entitled to a wry grin. Isn't that a description that could easily fit most of our wild country?

The outrageous Maiden Pap immediately entices you onwards, a lump of rock so out of kilter with the surrounding bogland that it looks as though it has been dropped here by mistake. Then Morven appears, peering over its shoulder, another steep and conical aberration. It's like walking through a miniature Monument Valley.

I came across a deer carcass, a victim of the harsh winter where food sources had lain buried under feet of snow. The bugs hadn't even had time to get to work. It wouldn't be the last. This had been a recurring theme over the past few weeks; during a traverse in Glenshee there had been a few bodies, perfectly preserved, as if they had settled down to sleep in a freezer. Now with the snow melt the body count was being revealed.

I reached the ruined house at Corrichoich; just beyond lay even older remains of an ancient settlement, sad reminders of hard lives long gone. The track ran out here. Now there was the small matter of a couple of kilometres of bog to tackle, but I was surprised to find the ground crisp and dry and the going easy. The Flow Country appeared to be having a day of rest.

Morven is of modest height but it looks massive from the foot of the climb, a constantly vertical ascent in heather and scree with no respite. I had to cross several boulder fields. They were short-lived but unstable. At one point, I felt my left leg jerk and slide as a rock rolled taking my foot with it. I didn't pay much attention at the time, my forward momentum firmly in control, but I would pay for this later.

It was four and half miles to the triple-topped Scaraben with a lot of tough terrain in between but again the mountain appears greater than the sum of its parts. I had put aside ten hours for this circuit but needed just seven.

I made a short stop at the clearance settlement of Badbea, another opportunity for the emotions to boil, and then another in Aviemore for food and a leg stretch. They certainly felt as if they could do with a stretch, one in particular. It seemed that innocent slip on Morven was beginning to exact a price. By the time I reached home, I was struggling to raise myself out of the car. My left leg felt as though it had locked. Now I had a new worry for the moon walk schedule. One panicked call to my physio next day, and I was lying on the padded table, hands gripping the bar above my head tightly while she stretched my leg down as far as it would with a towel wrapped my ankle for leverage. It seemed the slip that knocked my hip down a notch, taking it slightly out of alignment. I had ten days and another session or two to recover before heading off to Gairloch and Torridon.

§

IF the last thing I needed at this point was another long car journey, any real or imagined pains were wiped out when I arrived at the rental house. It sat a few miles to the west of Gairloch at Big Sand, the rooms split over three levels with the frontal glass panes dropping the full height of the building. There was an uninterrupted view south over the sparkling waters of Caolas Beag to Longa Island, but the jewel in the crown was the easterly aspect where the Torridon mountains were lined up on the horizon above Loch Gairloch.

When the sun shone, as it did most of that week, the light afforded by the glass walls was immense. But when the rain and wind were launching a full-frontal assault, the vibe was more of a beach house gone Gothic, and it wouldn't have felt out of place to have had The Phantom of the Opera knocking out a wee ditty from the third floor landing.

The first night in new surroundings is always a familiarisation, a leisurely dinner and a discussion of the mountain plans. This year we had the added bonus of a special cake and Champagne to celebrate one of our number completing her Munros the previous year, the first opportunity to get everyone in the one place since the big finish. I already had two of the group, Andy and Rebecca, keen to join me for the Beinn Eighe moonlight walk, but as the festivities rolled on a few others began to think maybe they could give it a go as well.

We always try to have a walk on the first day for the whole group. After that, everyone gets down to doing their own thing; some walk every day, some every other day, and with some it depends what the weather is doing. The next morning, the ten-strong group drove round towards Diabiag and assembled at the high point of the road. Despite the best efforts of the sun, there was still a bite in the air, a sign that winter might yet have a foothold in the higher reaches.

With the midnight walk later that night in mind, we had chosen the short route up to An Ruadh-mheallan as the communal leg-stretcher. This little gem of a hill allows a clear sight of the western aspect of Beinn Alligin, and was one of the options I had looked at – and quickly discarded – for the Wolf Moon walk in January. From this summit, you can take a northern then eastern line to walk right round Alligin, descending by the Bealach a' Chombla, but it's rough ground and in the dark with snow cover, it didn't seem the sensible choice.

We were back at base by early afternoon, the day now all

about resting up for the night expedition. Unsurprisingly, as the evening wore on and darkness fell, the enthusiasm from last night had begun to wane as the reality of the task ahead was laid out. It would be full winter gear, with axes and crampons; heavy packs and boots, no lightweight alternatives.

As one of the drop-outs said: "It sounded like a good idea at the time."

Our party stayed at three. I had no worries about my companions; Rebecca was an experienced walker with military training and had been out on a night expedition with me years before, on Ben Lomond for the summer solstice, while Andy was a caver, so crawling around in the dark would hardly be a problem. We sat out on the long porch in the late evening sun. The cloud had closed in over the Torridon peaks, the perfect view now vanquished. Baosbheinn had attracted a rainbow on its right flank, a sign there may be rain or even snowfall up there. It was a far cry from the evening before when the whole range lay pink in the sunset glow, the nearly full moon giving its blessing to the scene of calm. The next couple of hours were spent checking the cloud level. It seemed to be toying with us, sanctioning a glimpse of the summits one minute, then snatching them away again.

We hadn't bothered trying to catch any sleep. I have long learned that taking it easy is every bit as advantageous as trying to force yourself into unrequired sleep. We did load up on food, another big dinner before the main event. Time was passing slowly. We were ready to go, but we didn't want to go too early. In the end, the waiting got to us and we said our goodbyes like we were heading to the other side of the world.

The earlier weather hiccups seemed to have cleared. The moon was sending a shimmering corridor of light over every loch we passed, deep blue above, deep blue below, with a fuzzy strip of grey in the middle. It kept us company down the side of Loch Maree then round into Glen Torridon, a vibrant reflection on every dark slope.

It had been warm in the car but as soon as we stepped out, we felt the bite. We put on our head torches to dress and check our gear. It wouldn't be the first night walk where equipment was left lying beside the car, or, in one case, on the roof.

I asked Becks to pass my walking poles from the boot. She handed me three. It looked as if the change in sleep patterns had hit her already.

She looked at me: "What?"

"Since when did I have three arms?"

"Oh, sorry." Then the defence. "Well, you might have wanted to carry a spare."

I had strapping on both knees as a precaution. The rucksack seemed to weigh a ton. Not surprising when you reckon it held three cameras, including a big SLR, extra clothes in anticipation of the possible vast variation in temperature from night to day, ice axe, crampons, extra food, and cans of pink gin. Ah yes, the drink link. It was unlikely we would be sitting enjoying a tipple high on a ridge in below-zero conditions, but it's the thought that counts. Only Hannibal would be looking at inviting pink elephants along on a mountain crossing.

Beinn Eighe is not so much a mountain, more a range. It consists of two Munros, four Munro Tops and one Corbett on a ridge that runs almost 10km from Kinlochewe. The area was established as a National Nature Reserve in 1951, the first in the country, and covers more than 10,000 acres.

We set off just before 11pm. The moon was hanging over Sgurr Dubh at our backs, rendering head torches redundant on the initial gradual walk up the stepped Coire Dubh path. Liathach's dark walls loomed to our left, casting long, impenetrable shadows.

The pace of walking at night is always slower, a combination of the body adapting to the unsocial hours, the weight of the extra gear being carried, the need to be confident of every foot placement.

We plodded on, over short rocky rises, over the stepping stones fording the stream, past glittering pools with grasses standing to attention, frozen drips on every tip like a sea of miniature candles. We reached the cairn that marks the path split and headed right, now on bigger boulders, which take a curvature that leads eventual into Coire Mhic Fhearchair. As we turned the corner, the moonlight was temporarily snuffed out in the depths of this valley of leviathans and we had to revert to using the torches.

Off to our right, we spotted lights in the darkness, followed by movement. Deer, just feet away on the slope to our right, gleaming yellow eyes and visible puffs of breath turning them into creatures more suiting a nightmarish fairy tale. They were holding their ground, as puzzled by the unexpected appearance of the lights of three cyclops as we were by their unusual behaviour. During daylight hours, they wouldn't have hesitated to take flight. Now they were curious, and that curiosity seemed to have neutralised their natural instincts.

We climbed by a gently running stream to arrive in a corrie cast entirely in shadow. The slight ripple in the water was the only clue it was there. The Triple Buttress, those three mighty pillars which normally fill the eyeline on entrance, were missing. The moon occasionally managed to shine through over the ridge but it seemed so diluted by the drop in height the ground remained invisible.

On a wild night in March, 1951, a Lancaster bomber from RAF Kinloss flew into the Triple Buttress. The weather was so fierce that it was days before rescuers could reach the site, and months before the bodies of the eight men who had been on board were recovered. Debris still lies scattered around the foot of the buttress and in one of the gullies, which is known as Fuselage Gully.

That lack of light saw us lose the path in the boulder maze, so we decided to take a direct line to try to reach the stone chute in the far corner which leads to the main ridge. The topography was fooling us. We could see a long, dark ridge on our left behind which rose snow-dusted slopes. We set this as our target and pushed on, but we never seemed to get any closer. More steps upward, more minutes passing, still no joy. We stopped and huddled for a discussion. If it was an optical illusion, it was affecting the three of us. A few more steps, the same result. We got the map out and checked our position. We were right where we should be, hadn't strayed off course according to the readings. We could see the shining white slash of the gully we were aiming for so why did it seem we were making progress?

Then the penny dropped: the light that had been blanked out further down in the corrie was unencumbered further ahead, and it was casting a huge shadow of the Sail Mhor ridge behind us to the front. We had been trying to catch a moon shadow.

Suddenly, we couldn't get that song out of our minds. There was no doubt what the musical accompaniment to the Pink Moon was going to be. Moonshadow was written by Cat Stevens just before he decided he didn't want to be a feline any more, and its themes of hope, light in the darkest times and walking with only the moon for company seemed a decent fit.

Humming along in harmony, we reached the gully. Normally it's a scrambly inconvenience of an ascent, all broken rock and scree with slightly more secure steps off to the left. But the chimney was packed with old, hard snow. Someone had been up not so long ago but the steps they had kicked had filled in again with fresh snow, so we would have to re-kick our way up the steepening angle.

We didn't need crampons, just our axes as security. We kept a decent distance apart, mindful of the danger of loose rocks. We watched as one dislodged rock fired off sparks as it bounced and battered its way past us, a fireworks display that would have gone unnoticed in daylight. We emerged at the top of the chimney unscathed, but I suspected descending would be a different story. One slip and you could go a fair distance. Discretion was the watchword; it would be safer to commit to the full circuit.

I got the big camera out, only to discover the battery had worn down and it was now flat. Great. I had lugged all this gear along for more than three hours and it was just a dead weight. I was now carrying crampons and a big camera, neither of which would be needed.

The rise to the main summit of Ruadh-stac Mor was in fresh powder, gentle, yet we were starting to feel the effects of the constant push in these strange hours. The crest was lit from the western side by the moon and from the east by an orange, yellow and pink glow on the horizon, a tequila sunrise of a dawn approaching.

We returned to the col, the colours of the dawn continuing to creep ever higher. We had already agreed not to descend the chimney back into the corrie, but the route ahead over the top of Triple Buttress also looked as if it could present problems because of hard-packed snow. We started up, but when we came to a steeper section we went off on the diagonal. There were footsteps heading this way, but further on this route didn't look too clever either, huge black outcrops hanging with laden cornices. We backtracked on steep and slushy ground, taking a rising line to outflank the steep snow on the ridge and emerged on an easier rise to the main spine.

We strolled along the ridge, the glow strengthening behind us, the whole mountain lighting up. The moon sat proudly above the formidable pyramids of Liathach. They looked like the high points of an alien planet with the moon sitting just above the summits. All around the colours were changing with every step; copper, orange and pink sluicing over the slopes of Coire Ruadh-staca, a blue horizon switching to pink like litmus paper behind Liathach, then its tips burning like red-hot coals.

Our pace had slowed and we were continually stopping just to stand and stare. The slopes we had just left were catching the full force of the rising sun, glowing copper through the long steaks of white. The red sandstone here sits on top of Lewisian gneiss, some of the oldest rock in the world. Even in summer, the mountain tops have white caps due to the layers of quartzite, a pure, white sandstone.

The light was playing games, creating shapes among the rocks, gargoyles guarding these ancient lands. I pointed this out to Andy.

"Yeah, that one looks like Yosemite Sam."

I couldn't quite see it, but maybe that was down to my lack of imagination.

"Actually, now that I look closer, it's more like Deputy Dawg."

Ah, now I got it. The hallucinations must have started. Walking in the mountains at night can do that to you. The eyes play tricks, the constantly changing light twisting any sense of perception. I knew it well from experience; I have held conversations with trees, chatted to six-foot otters sitting at summit cairns and once failed to notice I was in the middle of a river. As if on cue, Becks piped up.

"Don't you think that looks like a giant sandcastle?" she said, pointing over at Liathach. I suppose it must have been affecting me as well now. It looked like she may have a point.

The hour between 3am and 4am is known as the witching hour or devil's hour, a time of night associated with supernatural events, when witches, ghosts and demons are said to be at their most powerful. One legend has it that women caught outside during this hour without good reason could be accused of witchcraft and executed. It's also often referred to as the death hour, the period when the most people die in their sleep. Double jeopardy for sleepy Becks then. I suggested she might want to make sure and stay awake for the rest of the walk.

We were now in the full light of morning. The second Munro summit, Spidean Coire nan Clach, its dark, crenellated rock towers in stark contrast to the blankets of deep, pristine white sweeping down its flanks, lay dead ahead. We were deep in the throes of exhaustion, and that peak just looked a few steps too far. The trig pillar which marked the start of the route off the mountain looked tempting. We had now been on the move for nearly eight hours, through the night and into the morning. Andy and I were torn; we both wanted to tick this second Munro but while the minds were willing, the bodies were weak. Becks had already decided she would sit it out at the trig. We sat with her for ten minutes, a bite of food and a bit of respite before the final push. The illusion of a long, high climb was just that and we were back at her side within 20 minutes.

All thoughts of hurrying down for an early breakfast had long passed; now we just wanted to bathe in the glory of this magnificent sunrise. Walking from the darkness into the light has that effect on even the weariest of mountaineers. The silence, the beauty, the privilege of seeing the birth of a new day never grows old.

We could have quite happily slept there, but eventually we dragged ourselves up and started the descent into Coire an Laoigh. The winter clothing was being stripped away piece by piece, a good excuse for more rest stops. As we neared the bottom of the corrie and hit the final stretch through the heather, we met a walker on the way up. We had a brief chat and warned him of the possible problems of an exit down the snow-stuffed chimney.

A few hundred metres further on and another group of walkers on the way up. It seemed the world had awakened while we only wanted to get some sleep. As we neared the end of the path, we spotted a car dropping someone off. Here was a chance to get a lift and avoid the extra couple of kilometres along the road.

Becks was out in front as we all started running while frantically trying to catch the driver's attentions. Just a few metres from the car, her foot sank into a hole and she went flying. I decided that catching that car was still the most important task, so vaulted over her prone form. Our ride now arranged, I was able to turn my attention to the walking wounded. The damage was worse than first thought; she was hobbling along with Andy's help with blood pouring down her leg, trousers badly torn. It seemed she may have been too premature in dismissing talk of a witch's curse.

We took it easy on the drive back to Gairloch, but much of the weariness had abated now we knew we were almost home. We were greeted as returning heroes by the rest of the clan, some four hours later than scheduled, having been on the hill for ten and a half hours.

There was still the small matter of the celebratory drink. No one fancied a pink gin at this time of the day, but there was a bottle of pink wine (yes, it was actually called that) and we polished it off between the three of us. Wine for breakfast; it evoked memories of a distant, wilder lifestyle, but I genuinely believed it would aid any attempts to get some sleep. It didn't. I sank into the semi-circle of huge couches and throws and managed a few cat naps in between staring out of the wall to ceiling windows overlooking the water. I felt as though I had turned the corner with the full moon project.

Fifth time lucky and my faith had been restored, a timely reminder that there is no finer mountain sensation than walking through the night into a new dawn.

6
Flower Power

FLOWER MOON

(Tuesday, May 29, 15.19)
***Mountain**: Ben Lawers, Beinn Ghlas*
***Soundtrack**: One Day I'll Go Walking – Deacon Blue*
***Celebratory drink**: Flowers Original Ale*

Mountain walking is supposed to be a supreme form of relaxation, a pastime that can wash away the cares of everyday life and reset the clock, but these full moon walks were proving the polar opposite. Although I felt I had turned the corner with the Pink Moon, the next walk would highlight a different set of stress factors.

May is the month when spring is firmly in control, when the remaining snowfields melt away at an ever increasing rate and the daylight hours stretch. There's a sense of awakening; the landscape has completed the switch from the muted pallors of winter to a riot of colour. Trees are approaching full foliage, wild flowers are carpeting the ground. Birdsong is all around, the buzz and hum of insects everywhere. There's no mystery as to why this moon is known as the Flower Moon. The spring transformation theme is prevalent in the alternative names too; Corn Planting Moon, Milk Moon and Hare Moon.

It also fell this year on May 29, Oak Apple Day. This was once an annual public holiday in England to commemorate the restoration of the monarchy in 1660, hence its other name, Restoration Day. It's not all sweetness and light, however. The Flower Moon was pivotal in the birth of the FBI, as related in the book, *Killers of the Flower Moon*, where a gruesome series of murders and land grabs in Oklahoma proved too much for the local police forces, with criminal tentacles spilling over state lines.

The Flower Moon is said to be the brightest moon of the year, so it was fitting this should be the night walk chosen to feature on BBC Scotland's *Landward* programme. Catch this perfectly and it would be a cameraman's dream.

The filming plans had come in a roundabout way. When the show made contact around a year earlier, they had been looking for a short filler feature about walking in the hills at night, based on my first book, *Moonwalker*. When we started chatting about the logistics – it was late autumn so we were running out of time – I mentioned that I was working on a new book.

Suddenly, there was a fresh impetus to the conversation. The idea of walking mountains on the nights of the full moon, and whose names correlated with those moons, had piqued the imagination. Forget the random night walk, this could now be a unique feature rather than a filler. We agreed to hold off until the spring. The walk would ideally take place in either April, May or June, a better chance of catching more hospitable weather. Also, by this time I would be three or four moons in, so we would have a good idea if everything was still going according to plan. Television filming schedules are tight, especially with a feature that is so weather dependent. We would just have to agree on a date that would suit all parties, and if there was any problem the chance was lost, probably for good. It wasn't unusual for planned filming of outdoors features to be abandoned.

My schedule was fixed, but the only full moon date that aligned with the rest of the crew was May 29. If there was low cloud, heavy rain, high winds, the film shoot would not take place. I didn't have the choice. No matter the conditions, it would be another night of wandering over the high tops on my own. It was now in the lap of the gods.

The one slight advantage was that the mountain chosen was Ben Lawers. Sitting more in the eastern half of the country, the odds that the night skies would be clear were statistically higher than if it had been in the west. It was a thin thread to cling to, but at least it was something.

Ben Lawers is the highest mountain in Tayside, the centrepiece of a chain of seven Munros sitting above Loch Tay. The area is a National Nature Reserve, owned and managed by the National Trust for Scotland with the support of Scottish Natural Heritage. It is famous for its alpine flora and attracts botanists from all over the globe. It was the only choice for the Flower Moon walk.

Despite almost touching 4,000ft, Ben Lawers is a busy mountain, the numbers swelled by casual walkers attracted by the relatively high starting point of nearly 1,500ft and an obvious path all the way to the top. The inevitable result of a good path and a not-too-strenuous walk is the creation of multiple ugly scars. With the passage of so many feet and so much delicate ground and plant life, the need for repair and regeneration to try to minimise the damage is constant.

Despite that, I have been on the mountain at times when

walkers were outnumbered by botanists. On one occasion we were sitting in the pub at Lawers, the only two walkers out of some 20 people in the bar. The rest had all been there for the plant life, some from as far as Switzerland.

I doubted we would encounter any walkers on the mountain in the dead of night. Or botanists, for that matter. The time and venue of the walk hadn't been advertised so it was unlikely there would be any attendant groupies either.

The conservation and protection work done here is a heartening success story. There are more rare mountain plants here than anywhere else in the country. There are more than 500 different types of lichens. There are mosses unique to this area; some restricted by natural processes, some by the human factor. Much of the damage to the grasslands is down to intensive farming methods over the centuries, in particular over-grazing by sheep and free-roaming deer. There are still sheep on the hill, but their number and movement is restricted.

An enclosed section, built in 1990 and combined with smart pathwork leading into, and out of, the immediate area, has led to the revival of many species of plant and wildlife. A raised path and boardwalk leads walkers over soft, boggy areas allowing the assorted bog mosses, heathers, cottons and asphodels to thrive unhindered. Once you step inside the enclosed area, the vegetation changes dramatically. It's an oasis of greenery.

The path meanders its way through a lush mix of trees, ferns and shrubs, alongside streams whose banks are covered by a riot of alpines, tall grasses and wildflowers. Stepping stones keep walkers to the correct line, avoiding heavy tread on delicate embankments and edges. Birdsong is everywhere, as is the buzzing of insects. Dragonflies, the helicopter gunships of the insect world, hover and dart. A natural order, decimated over the years, is returning. Insect-eating birds like whinchats and stonechats have recolonised the area, drawn by the abundance of food. Willow warblers and redpoll are here again in number. There is a huge variety in species of moth. Butterflies, including the often elusive mountain ringlet, are drawn in by the variety of flowers. Birds are not the only species thriving on this rich insect banquet; carnivorous plants such as butterwort and sundew have settled down here for a regular meal.

The steep slopes of a gorge offers protection to ledge plants like bitter vetch and to rowan and birch trees. Anemones, primrose, woodrush and ferns have spread too. Bilberry, crowberry and cowberry provide gaudy spots of interest. The overall result is a continual colour change from April to August, each plant having its moment in the sun; wonderful, evocative names like Devil's-bit scabious, procumbent pearlwort, purging flax, viviparous bistort, Marsh hawk's-beard, long-stalked yellow sedge.

There's more boardwalk leading over boggy ground to reach a gate emerging from the compound. The contrast is stark, the effects of man evident. The soil is poor, acidic. With the grazing restrictions, some regrowth is happening but it will be a long process. Further up Coire Odhair is a group of shielings, buildings used by graziers bringing their cattle up and down the track. The patches of brown on the front slope of Beinn Ghlas are peat beds, cut in earlier times, which continue to be eroded by the wind and rain. Time is a great healer though, and the overall picture is healthy. It would be wonderful if this success story could be emulated all over the country.

§

WITH the *Landward* arrangements in place, the stress factor kicked in. The rest of the month would be spent watching the weather forecasts, all the varying scenarios being screened inside my head. I had a one-track mind, plugged into an eight-track deck.

There's never any concern when I'm going solo. I plan what I am going to do and have two or three options in case I have to change. As soon as someone else is involved, it's a different story. The rules change, timings are compromised. The faffing fear is resurrected. The nagging doubts move in like rowdy gatecrashers at a party and the place is trashed. I shift the burden on to my shoulders. Now I am responsible for the whole party having a good time. Even the weather is down to me. I know it's not logical, but logic doesn't come into the equation. The responsibility is mine, and I won't enjoy the party until it's done and dusted and everyone has had a good time.

The *Landward* shoot wasn't the only show in town in May. The advance party for the proposed Canon promotional film had reported back and we had the green light for the middle of the month. The only worry around my new role as the emerging Johnny Depp of the mountains was the niggling knee injury which had threatened to derail the Pink Moon walk, but despite ten days' heavy duty walking in the north-west, there were no ill effects. If you can survive a day leaping and scrambling about on the towers of An Teallach with a supposedly dodgy knee, then there's little to worry about.

The three-strong Canon film crew arrived on the Monday evening, and we shot some interiors, my daughter's house passing off as a newspaper office. This was the start of the *Moonwalker* story; working in the office late at night, then switching off the computer, and heading out of the door supposedly on the start of a dark journey to distant mountain ranges.

Next morning we were off at the crack of dawn to our hotel base near Oban, where we caught up with two more members of the team. Mid-afternoon and the whole team drove round to Glencoe village and then along to the start of the walk up the Pap of Glencoe.

This had been chosen by the recce team and myself as the best peak for a night climb, rather than one of the more famous giants of the glen. It was short and sweet, ideal for a group of non-mountaineers struggling with heavy camera and sound equipment. It also commands a glorious view west from Loch Leven and Loch Linnhe to Ardgour in one direction, while east there was the massed ranks of the Mamores rising up from the waters and woods of the shoreline.

We set off around 5pm, grey clouds massing in the distance, but it was all threat, no action. The biggest worry wasn't the possibility of rain, it was the thought that the views from the summit would be shrouded in mist. Progress is slow when climbing a hill for filming. Every glint of sunshine, every pass of running water, is a photographic opportunity. All the gear has to be unpacked, set up in the right position and then there are several takes from different angles. You can climb the same section of ground half a dozen times. Then everything has to be carefully packed away again.

It's stop-start for the first couple of hours and little height is gained. What would normally be a climb of just over an hour and a half had stretched to double that by the time we were approaching the rocky summit. The light had been fading bit by bit and now we were left with just a late polish on the steely water in the distance. The cloud had stayed high and the views were expansive but it seemed we were in an old black and white movie, a far cry from the flashy colour extravaganza needed to plug a new camera.

That old chestnut of leading a group into disappointment was starting to make itself known, the best of Scotland destined to remain hidden to these visitors. The cold was beginning to bite. The cameras were primed, the crew trying their best to duck down into sheltered spots out of the chill wind. Then off to our right, a burst of light through the grey, a last hurrah from the sinking sun. Some heavenly intervention – the shoot had been rescued. The sun dropped further but the colours kept coming, a perfect celestial sandwich; pink and purple stripes at the top, orange and yellow threading through deep grey cloud on the horizon, and a filling of brilliant white light, the parting shots of the sun.

We were there for three hours. Fingers were numb, noses were running. It was time to get off the hill. Descending a mountain in the dark is always the most tense part of the walk. Descending with a bunch of under-equipped novices ramps up the anxiety levels. Reaching the final cone of Sgurr na Ciche involves a bit of hands-on work through a boulder field, all wobbling rocks and loose scree, but climbing up is relatively simple. Coming down is a different story, the potential for a slip on the unstable terrain heightened. It didn't help that some of the footwear was unsuitable to a long walk around a shopping centre, never mind a mountain. It took a while, and a bit of hand-holding and foot placement, to get everyone down to easier ground.

The sky continued to produce fireworks on the descent, luminescent streaks of green and orange taking turns to provide the backdrop with the twinkling lights of Ballachulish and the bridge far below. There were a few film stops on the way down, and the darkness and loose ground added to the ponderous pace but there was no way to speed things along. The main concern was getting everyone down to the road safely.

We arrived back at the cars by 2am and the hotel an hour later, managed to grab three hours' sleep and breakfast in a brown bag before we were back on the road to the Pap. There had been two more arrivals overnight, swelling the group size to seven. The morning conversations turned a bit corporate as the new faces got up to speed; I was grateful to be the outsider, just along for the ride. There was a bit of whispered progress talk overheard. It seemed our night trek and the boulder field in particular had taken some of the group way beyond their comfort zone.

"How did it go on the mountain last night?"

"Well, imagine the walks we do down south are rated as one out of ten for difficulty."

"Okaaaay."

"Well the climb last night started off as a four, and ended up as a nine."

"Oh, right."

"It got worse. It was a definite ten plus on the way down."

At least we would be on the hill in daylight this time. We didn't venture too far up, instead focusing on the final descent in the sunshine. And then came the call I had been waiting for:

"We need to take some shots of your feet."

Where would any mountain shoot be without close-ups of boots splashing through water, over boulders and on muddy paths? Pay close attention the next time you watch any outdoor footage – the feet reign supreme. I have been involved in a few shoots over the years and my feet have always been given star billing over my face. Some of you may not be surprised at that, but it is true with everyone, no matter how morphologically challenged they might be.

I reckon if this goes on, my feet should get an agent and go their own way.

The final shots in the bag, we drove back east and did some more home filming with my oldest granddaughter Ava. By this time, a sound engineer had arrived and we did an interview, followed by another modelling shoot for Ava with a different photographer, before heading out in the dark again to film some driving scenes on back country roads. The next day was spent on nearby Kinnoull Hill to capture some of the camera's features in action. A team of ten, over a total of six days, to arrange and shoot a film that lasted around two minutes, and the only damage was to the psyche of some who had clambered up a wee peak at the end of Glen Coe. Result.

I was fresh out of laurels, no time to rest on them anyway. Another crack of dawn start, this time heading to Ardrossan for the ferry to Arran and four days of the island's mountain festival. This would be my fourth year in attendance. The first year I was there as the main speaker, and I was then invited back to lead a night walk on Goatfell as part of the programme. Somewhat surprisingly, this proved so popular that we had to extend it to two nights to contend with the waiting list. Who knew there were so many people willing to pay to go walking in the hills at night? It has become a regular event and is fully booked every year.

The weather had been remarkably kind the previous two years. The nights have always been cold and moonlight unpredictable, but the sight of the rising sun always warms everyone. I suppose we had to run out of luck. The Goatfell walk went well, the best weather so far, the red tips of the sun burning its way through a sea of orange holding everyone transfixed, but on the second night, we had rain and wind and no chance of a view. Eight had booked, but with just a few minutes to departure, none had turned up. I had thought it likely no one would want to go out on a night like this, and Rachael, the mountain guide for the night, thought likewise. Just when we thought we would have a night off, two of the eight appeared, ready and willing to do the circuit. It proved to be a long night. It was also bad timing that Towel Day was still a few days away – we certainly needed a few by the finish.

The upside was that just two days later we were treated to the start of a mini heatwave. I joined friends for a Cairngorms jaunt, the long, hot walk on to Beinn a' Bhuird from Linn of Quoich. There were still large remnants of the winter cornices hanging precariously, but they were in their final throes. The panic that the Arran monsoon was a harbinger of unsettled conditions had subsided; it looked increasingly likely the Ben Lawers walk with the Landward crew would happen.

§

HEADING along the lochside on the Monday evening with the sun going down in an explosion of pastel pinks and oranges, the fall-out washing over the calm waters. I reached the car park by 10pm, the sky still clear and bright. The Flower Moon was rising, gaining in strength with every single click of darkness. It looked as though it was determined to hold on to its crown as the brightest of the bunch.

There were a few vehicles dotted around, a few late evening strollers taking their time before they had to turn their backs on this rare example of a Scottish paradise. I took a short stroll, and raised my head to the mountains as if giving my seal of approval. You can afford to do that when the midges are not out in force. The silence, the peacefulness, was intoxicating. The BBC team of four arrived from their base nearby 15 minutes before midnight, director Kirsty, production co-ordinator Susan, cameraman David and presenter Dougie Vipond. There was an infectious air of excitement. We were like kids who had been allowed a curfew extension to stay out to play.

The moon was a huge, brilliant white shiny penny dominating the sky. At this time of year and with a perfect sky, there is almost perpetual light and the jagged silhouette of the skyline to the north with its deep blue infill was a hint that there wouldn't be a long wait until a new dawn. We had the lights, we had the cameras and now it was time to provide the action. A short moonlit scene-setter in the car park with Dougie and then the five of us were off on the boardwalks and stone steps of the restored track heading for the black ridge looking ahead.

The walk up to Ben Lawers goes over another Munro, Beinn Ghlas, and takes just over two and a half hours. That's not film crew time, though. We had something like four hours to reach the Lawers summit for the sunrise at 4.38am. There's no reprise if you arrive a few seconds too late; we had to make sure we didn't miss the moment.

We crossed the boardwalk over the bog, then passed through the enclosed area following the Edramucky Trail, the heat already starting to stifle, sweat pouring from our brows. It was a relief to come out of the trees on to the open hill, audibly sighing en masse when the cool breeze blew a kiss across our faces.

The conversation with Dougie up to this point had focused on my search for a suitable soundtrack for this walk. I reckoned if I had a genuine musical star alongside me I should make best use of that opportunity. Song titles were thrown back and forward, but nothing seemed to fit. There were plenty of flower-based songs, and the usual plethora of moon titled pieces, but in the end it seemed fitting to use something from Deacon Blue. The next phase of the chat was for the camera. We had stopped at a cluster of boulders just where the path split at the mouth of Coire Odhar. This was the first filming and interview stop before we started the climb in earnest. The moon was helping out with the lighting. Dougie asked me about the book, the unusual pattern of full moons this year and how I had made my mountain choices to match each moon. Then we did a few takes with the two of us walking up the path, together and individually. The real stars of the show, our feet, got their own segment as usual.

We plodded up the zig-zags, no stopping until we crested the ridge where the landscape opened. Ahead of us was the squat shape of Beinn Ghlas, with a grey line of low mist under pre-dawn stripes of red, pink and orange stripes, topped with a lone, wispy cloud shaped like a tadpole. At our backs, the moon was still pulsing high above the cluster of pinprick lights in Killin. We took a few shots in either direction plus the hikers' equivalent of a flypast, then moved on

Dougie pointed out some strange coloured lights moving across otherwise dark terrain midway between the moon and the loch. They were moving in strange patterns, and quickly, like alien spacecraft quartering the hillsides for signs of life. There didn't seem to be any rational explanation. I half expected to see Elliott cycling across the face of the moon, E.T. sitting in the front basket. We were also treated to the sight of a shooting star streaking across the night sky. There was a whole celestial circus going on above us.

We reached the summit of Beinn Ghlas to find the skyline ahead filled with the massive dark bulk of Ben Lawers. The early colours that formed the backdrop had risen further but in doing so seemed to have lost some of their intensity, now more of a pastel wash.

Poor Beinn Ghlas. It is one of those hills that suffers from being such in close proximity to a mightier neighbour. It would be easy to stroll past its summit without thinking. Even the cairn has that can't-be-bothered look, a small jumble of stones which spills down the side of the hill, yet in another place it would be a significant mountain, one of the higher Munros. Location really is everything.

David positioned himself further on the path and then asked Dougie and myself to go back down Beinn Ghlas and then come walking over the summit again with the moon appearing to push us on. We did a couple of takes but I couldn't honestly claim three ticks for Beinn Ghlas. I know someone who would though. The camera gear was packed away and divided among the group for the final push but we only seemed to have gone a few steps when David started salivating about another, better, view and sequence. Out came the gear again and we did a few takes walking on the path from Beinn Ghlas, the moon now a ball of white fuzz, a lightbulb wrapped in cotton wool, sitting perfectly between the triangles of two peaks.

This latest filming stop had shrunk our remaining time dramatically. The question was asked: How long to the summit? Forty minutes. How much time do we have until sunrise? Forty minutes. No more interruptions, it was now a non-stop dash to the top.

There was no time to change gear, to shrug off the extra layers we had donned when standing about earlier. The slight chill we had felt at the last stop was burned off immediately on the push up the steep final slope. I was roasting. This was full sweat-al jacket. David was out in front, as if realising he might miss the sunrise money shot. He was carrying the bulk of the camera gear and his pace was starting to slow with every step. The top was starting to feel further away. I was close behind, Dougie a bit behind me. Susan and Kirsty were further back still. I caught up with David and took the tripod. I put it vertically across my shoulders and charged on. His load lightened, David now regained his step. I hit the summit with five minutes to spare, probably a few pounds lighter due to the sauna operating inside my jacket. David appeared a few seconds later, immediately getting his tripod and camera into position by the trig pillar. I had gone further over to the huge cairn and when Dougie appeared he headed straight there as well. Susan and Kirsty made it up just in time to catch the first glimpse of the burning red crown on the horizon.

We watched as the sun came up fast, changing from red to deep gold to yellow to brilliant white, every stunning second caught on film. The cairn and trig point looked like prehistoric totems when lit starkly from below by the fierce brilliance of the light. The landscape was coming alive all at once, a 360 degree shift from night to day.

The beauty of such a simple event is immeasurable, and it's always fascinating to watch the reactions of those around you during this transformation. Dougie couldn't drag his eyes away. David was in his element, changing position to catch every possibility. Kirsty and Susan were torn between their production duties and snatching every glimpse of the light show they could.

David launched the camera drone and we had to stay in place for the next ten minutes as it buzzed overhead, reducing us to tiny, insignificant figures in the landscape. Despite the spring feel, the extremities were starting to feel the early chill, and we were happy when we could drop down just below the summit to find a shelter out of the wind for the final interview. As we chatted, lenticular cloud formations kept up the alien theme, giant spaceships forming faultless curves over the tops of the mountains to the east.

With the final scenes and conversation wrapped, it was time for breakfast. I had thought all the heavy packs had contained camera and sound gear. That was until Dougie opened his. He was carrying for four, and it had been packed for every eventuality. There was certainly no danger they would go hungry – I had never seen so much food for so few people on the hill. It looked as if they had carried out a ram raid on a supermarket.

We bypassed Beinn Ghlas, cutting across its slopes and down into Coire Odhar to rejoin our outgoing route, the sun now blazing down. We met a few early risers on their way up, all with that slightly questioning look at this party descending from the mountain with a mix of weariness and satisfaction on their faces. I had originally planned to spend more time examining and photographing some of the plant life in daylight, but the little people operating my body were having none of it. We had done the night shoot, and now the credits had rolled. All I could do now was wait for the BAFTA committee to call.

7
In the Heat of the Night

STRAWBERRY MOON

(Thursday, June 28, 05.53)
Mountain*: Mam Sodhail, Carn Eighe,*
Beinn Fhionnlaidh
Soundtrack*: Strawberry Fields Forever – The Beatles*
Celebratory drink*: Fruli strawberry beer*

We walked into the sunset leaving the last of the day's light further behind with every step. There were no fireworks over the distant western mountain skyline, just a sallow wash, but it was achingly beautiful all the same. This was the civil hour at its most imperious.

The waters of Loch Affric lay perfectly still recovering from a hard day in the heat, the huge ridges of the mountain horseshoe around us fading to a charcoal backdrop. The walk along the shore was accompanied by that silence that's never quite silent; lone bird calls, the occasional buzz or whirr of a passing insect staying up past its bedtime and the gentle dribbling and gurgling of gently running water.

As yet, there was no sign of the Strawberry Moon. This

was the seventh full moon of this extraordinary year of full moons, and I had the company of Grampian Club mates Pauline and James to walk around the Affric summits behind Strawberry Cottage, the mountaineering hut which sits on the track at the western end of Loch Affric.

The cottage was a disappointment. I had remembered it as painted white, perfect for a picture with the dark mountains as a backdrop with the moon providing the flash. But it was dark green and with the sun below the horizon, almost invisible in its surroundings.

I wondered if we would have any real darkness at all. It was nearly midnight yet the path ahead was clear, the colours of the surrounding slopes and pinpricks of water still radiating. Then, just as we reached the bridge for the turn north into the shadows of Coire Ghaidheil, we caught our first sighting, a glowing white crown on the skyline behind. The throbbing rays of light pushing their way through the deepest of the darkness was appreciable, the monochrome battle ground of the corrie starkly captured.

The moonlight illuminating the way ahead meant there was no need for torches until we reached the deeper shadows camouflaging a section of boggier ground near the final rise. A left turn on the path would lead to An Socach, a mini-Munro squeezed into this land of the giants. We turned right and headed steadily up over stonier ground, a gentle angle continually on the rise. The moon was circled by a yellow ball of fuzz, and for the first time we felt a chill, a light breath of wind homing in on the wet spots on our base layers. The path stayed on a lazy trajectory, taking its time on the long traverse over the dark western slopes hugging the side of Creag Coire nan Each.

It continued coiling round imperceptibly until the massive beehive cairn of Mam Sodhail came into view, standing proudly on the skyline like a far-off castle waiting for an onslaught, an orange line on the eastern horizon signalling the infant stirrings of another day.

An until now unseen boulder field provided one last surprise as we made our way along the edge of a plunging, craggy neckline which denied us a direct approach before we reached the col for the final push up the ridge. The ruins of the old weather station just beneath the summit were picked out from the sweep of the dark mountainside by the increasingly flourishing light.

It brought back memories of an ascent of this mountain on an Alpine spring day, a steep snow climb out of Coire Leachavie which saw us needing to kick steps on the final escape to the ridge. The combination of snow and wind was proving too much for some and we ducked down into the ruined building to try to get some respite. We needn't have bothered. The snow had had taken full advantage of the lack of a roof and was piled to the tops of the walls. We looked a pathetic sight pushing aside the white stuff to try to squeeze in. Now you could pick out every line, every rock.

We sat under the castle walls and had a 2am breakfast, the moon restored to a perfect white orb, the skies ahead lightening by the second. For the first time since we had started, we were wearing an extra layer, the inevitable consequence brought on by sitting on a mountain top in the middle of the night. We stayed there for half an hour watching the battle between night and day, enjoying the moonlit silence, no rush to move on. By the time we left for the short up and down to the semi-detached neighbour Carn Eighe, the night had tipped into day.

Out to the north lay the final summit, Beinn Fhionnlaidh, a mountain that produces an equal share of expletives and superlatives. It always feels like a long drop down from the main ridge, and an even longer climb back. We were 45 minutes from sunrise so it required a fair dash. In contrast to the muted sunset, this was going to be spectacular. The sky seemed to be on fire, blazing oranges, reds and yellows the warm-up act for the sun king.

James, being of a much earlier vintage, had no problems making it in the requisite time. Pauline and I were a little behind schedule and were prepared to accept second best, but luckily for us the mountain horizon employed blocking tactics which produced a kind of delayed transmission from the heavens so we captured the moment nonetheless. Suddenly the mountains were bowing to the power of the new day. It was reminiscent of a smelter being fired up, the intensity of the colour coming from a sudden fury of deep lit kilns. Loch Mullardoch was a silver, well-fed python slithering contentedly through the contours. The moon hadn't given way just yet either. Its radiance was certainly fading to the west but it remained a perfect circle drifting above the nearby heights of Sgurr nan Ceathreamhnan and Mullach na Dheiragain, elegantly taking its time to exit the party.

The show was over, but we waited in impossible hope for an encore we knew would never come. The curtain had dropped on another spectacular and all we had left was the long way home. The big cairn on Mam Sodhail, such a welcoming sight on the way in, now took on the mantle of a malignant presence in the distance, merely a reminder of the weary slog ahead. Even the relief felt at reaching it again was tempered by the distance still to travel in the building heat and the walk along the shore seemed to go on forever.

Twelve hours on the hill, a sunset, a full moon and a sunrise included. Not a bad circular route.

§

IT may seem curious to have breakfast at 2am, but when you are committed to walking mountain circuits during the wee, small hours everything is going to be turned on its head. Sleeping and eating patterns are adjusted to take advantage of weather windows.

I often have porridge at 9 or 10pm, but does that make it breakfast? If it does, what would you call the intake session at 7am? Lunch? Another stop on the drive home around midday would count as dinner, or as we Scots say, 'yer tea'. The big advantage is that if you are climbing again the next day, you are in the market for two suppers, one at 5pm, the other at 10pm. It may all seem a bit mad, but you just have to imagine you are playing by Australian rules and the day is turned on its head.

You can add to this the constant snacking to make up for the amount of calories burned during an average walk, although this is relatively recent innovation in my case. When it comes to food on the hill, I have to admit I am a changed man. Friends used to find it astonishing that I would never eat, even during the longest mountain days. I never felt the need. As long as I was taking in plenty of fluids, I was okay. Besides, stopping for food breaks just wasted travelling time as far I was concerned: I could be on the next mountain in the time it took to stop and have lunch.

And when the weather is bad? Who wants to sit and eat a sandwich in pouring rain?

I did always carry a couple of Mars Bars tucked away in my bag in case of emergency. I still do, although often I would find them years later, the chocolate turning white from age. No worries though, I actually liked the albino version. The change is known as a fat bloom and is caused by liquid fat like cocoa butter oozing through the chocolate and crystallizing on the surface. It doesn't do any harm.

I learned this from a chocolatier I met on the Cuillin ridge (honest!), and when I told him I actually liked his product when it turned white he laughed and then said: "We hate people like you. You are supposed to throw it away then buy more."

(Note to self: Pitch for new TV show – The Hillwalking Dead. What happens when a couple of mountaineers feast on out of date chocolate?)

Anyway, I've seen the light (lunch). I have become an eating machine. It's snack, snack, snack all the way round. Still not so keen on sitting in the rain, though. The improvement in outdoor food products has also helped. Changed days from when most energy bars tasted like blocks of dried sawdust, although I still prefer a three-year-old Mars Bar.

I do have one eating ritual which often garners looks of curiosity from fellow walkers. Any time I am about to eat a filled roll, I always open it up and give it a final once over before ramming commences. This dates back to my student days when I worked weekend night shifts at a baker's in Dundee. I was one of a team involved in the mass production of morning rolls. It was a small, elite band, sort of like the A-Team had they been in the business just for the dough.

There was one person to measure out and mix the ingredients, operate the mixer, then wrestle the massive blob out of the machine and on to a metal table. He would chop it into smaller pieces and feed it into a dough dividing machine known as a Winkler. This split the dough into 24 cupcake sized pieces at a time, all perfectly aligned in four rows of six. They would pass through scalding steam and emerge from the other side puffed up to normal roll proportions, and we would be ready with a tray to catch them as they dropped, still in perfect formation. The trays would be then be put on a large trolley and wheeled into another steam bath, before being baked in the ovens.

The Winkler was a masterpiece of German engineering, operating flawlessly for decades. The same couldn't be said of us. One of the employees was a German man of indeterminate age. Herbie could have been 50 and had a hard life or he could have been 80, also having had a hard life. His English was non-existent, 'nein' and 'ja' were pretty much the scope of his conversational skills. Mind you, our Dundonian tongues also hinted at a lack of proper English, so maybe he thought we were from some strange land like Middle Earth. I always suspected he had been a free gift from the makers of the machine or that he had been a rough sleeper who had taken refuge unnoticed in Germany and simply fell out of the box when it arrived in Scotland.

Our dough man was a bit of a nervous wreck, always under pressure. Timing was everything on his production line. He was mixing one dough, spinning another and cutting yet another. When the yeast overdose threatened to overwhelm him, he would nip out for a cigarette and ask us to hold the fort. We enjoyed the opportunity to wrestle the dough out of the machine. It was like fighting Big Daddy, good practice for getting to grips with a large, amorous woman. Before you start getting outraged, consider the female clientele coming into an all-night baker and chowing down on a hamburger roll or a mega sausage roll at 3am. No skinny lattes here. We would often have ladies rolling around on the floor with the guys, punching lumps out of each other.

One night when the dough man had done his vanishing act, one of the other guys managed to manhandle the dough out and slam it down on the table. He then proceeded to chop it up and feed it into the machine. When John Dough returned he was pleased to see the table was clear. Until, that is, he couldn't find his cigarettes and matches.

"Where did you leave them?"

"On the dough table."

Now they were distributed throughout a few hundred rolls. He was distraught.

"What am I going to do?"

"Well, you could choose any one of these rolls and smoke it," was the unhelpful suggestion from the stand-in dough chopper. And that's why you should always carefully examine a roll before you eat it.

No one else was ever any the wiser and the brawlers at the front counter would get rolls that night which would also satisfy their nicotine habit.

The perks of the job meant getting six freshly baked rolls, still warm, at the end of the shift and armed with those and a pint of milk each, we would head up to the local football pitches and enjoy a kickaround by the light of the moon or under the rising sun.

§

JUNE had evolved into an exceptionally busy month. We had slipped into a long, settled spell with temperatures constantly hovering just below 30C, and I was due to be the road solid for eight days, so planning for the Strawberry Moon walk was bound to require a thorough food and drink agenda.

The month had started with a 13-hour run round six of the Mamores in searing heat as I helped drive my pal Rebecca's Munros to-do list down from seven to one. It was so hot that I took the unusual step of jettisoning virtually everything I usually carried in my rucksack to fill it with as much fluid as possible. Her face was a picture all day long; black with thousands of dead midges drowned in sweat at 9am, a mixture of joy and emotion on the final peak eight and half hours later where she couldn't even manage to produce a tear due to dehydration. We made it back to the pub just in time to get fed, and I managed to down three pints of cider in under 20 minutes without feeling any effect.

The following day I endured another tough round laced with constant drinking above Loch Eil. It was slow going with one particular rough ascent but the only perturbing aspect was what I found in the remote Glensuileag bothy, where someone had spent considerable time scrawling rambling, threatening, racist messages on torn-off strips of newspaper. It could have been an unpleasant night for anyone unfortunate enough to have had to share the shelter.

A couple of pleasant hill days in Galloway followed, then a gloomier ascent of Gulvain when two previous days of heavy rain proved too much for the dried-out ground. It was akin to walking down the middle of a river. One week later and it was out to Beinn Narnain at Arrochar for Rebecca's Munro 'compleation' party, a day in which you could see the cloud cover dialling back by the hour. We were heading for part two of the heatwave, just in time for the grand tour.

The Strawberry Moon had presented me with a few options. A Tayside boy, I could opt for a mountain that brought back memories of my berry-picking days in Angus and Perthshire. There were no Munros with a name that evoked the strawberry link. There was a Corbett, Meall nan Subh, the 'hill of the raspberry', near Glen Lyon, but it was the wrong category and wrong berry. There was also the old rule applied by many Scottish hillwalkers – when the weather is good all over the country, always head west. With that, the mountaineers' base of Strawberry Cottage popped into my head. I could circuit the mountains above the house in Glen Affric, as many or as few as the weather and fitness allowed.

No sooner had the venue been decided, the soundtrack kicked in. Again, there was choice but no direct link, and by this time I couldn't get Strawberry Fields Forever out of my head. The Beatles had another No.1.

As for a drink, I was spoiled. This was a moon that could get you bladdered. There was strawberry wine, strawberry beer, strawberry vodka, even strawberry whisky. I don't know why a beautifully produced drink made in Scotland made me feel slightly uneasy. I have seen people drinking hair lacquer mixed with milk, so it's puzzling that a whisky infused with strawberries should made me think twice. Perhaps it was because I was told I would be pleasantly surprised, and I had been told that years ago about a blind date. I settled for the beer, bought enough for my guests and stashed them in the rucksack. The bottles of beer, that is, not my friends. I had a couple of diversions before Glen Affric, so we arranged a time and place three days' from now.

First up was another television date, this time for a Dutch outfit. They were fascinated by the Munros and had contacted the Munro Society to take part in a three-part special about Scotland. It was a 4am Monday morning rise to meet the team of four from 3 op Reis Travel TV at the foot of Buachaille Etive Mor. The presenter was Geraldine, a former model who had moved into television on the Dutch version of *Blue Peter* before progressing to this holiday show. Her style was all-action and we walked up into the corrie and did a bit of light scrambling which looked good for the cameras. We spent around six hours on the mountain doing the interview, scrambling around with cameras running from all angles, including drone footage. And, of course, my feet

The rocky towers of mighty Liathach glowing red under the Pink Moon

The last sighting of the Wolf Moon during blizzard on Beinn Alligin

Beinn Alligin's white slopes after descent as storm starts to move in

View into the Northern Corries of Cairn Gorm

Under the walls of Coire an t-Sneachda as light fades

The Blue Moon on the early ascent of Bla Bheinn

Bla Bheinn looking benign during the day's recce

Liathach in a blue mood under the Pink Moon from Beinn Eighe ridge

Pink Moon, pink mountains – Torridon peaks from Gairloch

First sunlight on the faces of Beinn Eighe

The Flower Moon in its final throes over Beinn Ghlas

Sunrise from the summit of Ben Lawers

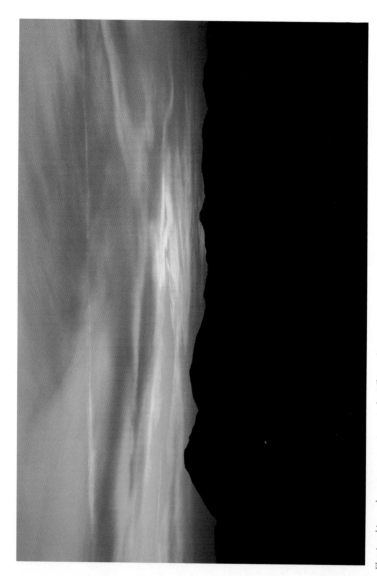

Flaming skies as the sun starts to rise over the Affric peaks

Strawberry Moon over Sgurr nan Ceathreamhnan

Strawberry beer for the
Strawberry Moon

Full moon on
Mam Sodhail

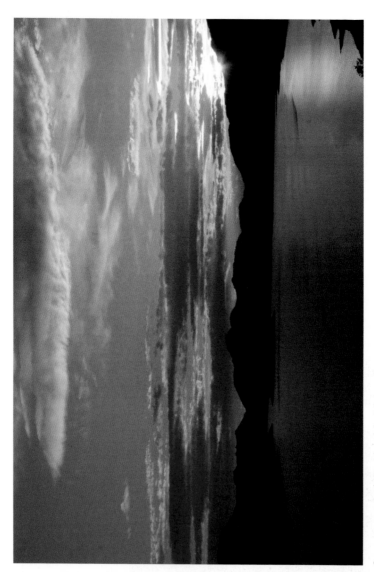

Sun setting over Loch Quoich and the Arkaig peaks

Buck Moon on the loch over Gairich

Morning sun glow over Arkaig hills

Approaching dry land after paddle across Loch Etive

Threatening skies as darkness falls on ascent of Ben Starav

A fleeting glimpse of the Harvest Moon on Beinn a' Ghlo

Stunning skies on morning descent of Beinn a' Ghlo

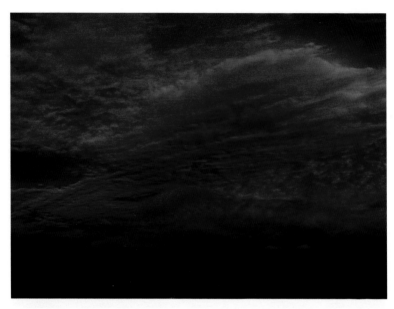

Alien skies during the ascent of Lochnagar

Wild conditions on the summit plateau

Happy faces despite the snow on top of Ben Cruachan

Golden teardrops from the Cold Moon on Ben Hope

Cold night, Cold Moon – the perfect finale on Ben Hope

got the film star treatment once again. At this rate, they will be moving to L.A. and dating Taylor Swift.

The original plan had been for two mornings' shooting, but the weather was so perfect we managed to wrap it all up in one lengthier session. That gave me the scope to fit in another walk before I was due to be at Invergarry, my base for the night. I decided to head for Meall Blair, the furthest west of three Graham peaks on the north side of Loch Arkaig. Multiple roadworks and heavy traffic around Fort William saw the clock ticking down. Then there was the never inconsequential matter of the long, twisting road along the lochside, and the fact that recent hydro work has changed the landscape so the start of the walk was difficult to find at the first attempt.

I wondered if I should abandon the attempt for another day. Then I remembered I would have to drive in here again on this rollercoaster road from hell and just went for it. The heat was intense, but the climb was fast, and I was on the summit in under an hour and a half. As I crested the penultimate hump, a long line of deer were trotting along the horizon in formation, startled by my unexpected arrival.

The views were sublime; the Corryhully and Arkaig Munros standing in retreating shades of blue above the head of the loch, late sunlight turning the waters a shimmering silver, and the seemingly endless swathes of bog cotton swaying like miniature candy floss in perfect harmony.

I made it in time to the hostel, then it was off early again next morning, the scenic drive through Glen Shiel and over the Mam Ratagan pass into Glenelg. Beinn a' Chapuill may be of modest height, but from the road past the Pictish brochs it starts to look formidable, a long ridge rising in a series of steps. The first obstacle came in the form of a bovine roadblock on the track past the farm, the cows and calves stretched out enjoying the unyielding sun. The lady at the farm smiled and waved and shouted over that her animals were docile but I remembered that old adage: let sleeping cows lie. A swift bypass and I was into mixed woodland, dappled light and shade, a cuckoo's incessant call and the constant purr of dragonflies. A rickety suspension bridge, hidden from view, gave access to an overgrown path and then open hillside. Beinn a' Chapuill is one of those hills that never seems to get any closer; every new rise a cruel trick. The summit area is obscure as well, lots of possible spots vying for the highest point, but at least with the perfect visibility it was easier to be sure.

My journey continued to Beauly to stay with friends, a great jumping off point for the Affric moon adventure. I had only been on the road for two days, but the effort so far made it feel more like I had spent two weeks lost in the woods, such was the weary, weather-beaten, dishevelled figure that appeared at their door.

I was meeting Pauline and James in Cannich at 5pm the following day for dinner or supper or wherever the hell we were at on the food rota now. Most of the day was spent eating and lazing around. I arrived at the pub just as South Korea were pulling off one of the biggest World Cup shocks in years by beating the holders, Germany, much to the chagrin of the elderly couple sitting in the ringside seats wearing their national team shirts.

Glen Affric is regarded by many as the most beautiful in Scotland but over the last few years there have been major run of river hydro works going on and the constant passage of heavy lorries and machinery has taken its toll. The road has been widened, the verges have been crushed, and the roadside vegetation severely chopped back. New tracks have been gouged out of the landscape, and there are ugly scars everywhere. It will be a long time before the landscape recovers. We drove cautiously along the winding road in the blinding light of the low sun, the flow of works traffic coming the opposite way creating a dodgems-style hazard. It was a relief to reach the busy main car park. We agreed on a 9pm departure and then went back to our vehicles to try to catch a couple of hours' sleep, without success in my case.

The heat had hardly abated since midday, and it was stifling in the car. The one advantage was there were no midges, the heat and the light proving too much for them. Pauline and James were able to lie out in the back of his van and keep the doors open. Two hours of restless sleep evasion later, and I was pulling on the boots. I envied the other pair their ability to drop off. I was used to going without sleep, however. They would pay for this later, I thought/hoped. If my throat hadn't been so dry, an evil laugh would have been forthcoming.

I had no worries about either of them on the hill at night. Pauline has walked all the Munros and done much more since, including ascents of Tower Ridge and some of the hairier Skye scrambles. She had also been out with me on night walks before. James was young and fit, and working towards his mountain leader badges.

Twelve hours later we would be back here. It was just after 6am when we dropped into the massive expanse of Coire Leachavie, the encircling faces providing some protection from the sun. The descent was slow and involved a few food stops – I had lost count; I think this would probably be next day's dinner if anyone had been keeping a tally – but that was no great hardship. It was comfortably warm, we were still in the shade, and the midges were still notable by their absence. I think there was also an unspoken group decision to avoid coming out into the full glare of the sun too soon. We passed a tent at one point, no sign of life.

By the time we hit the path along the shore, there was no longer any way to avoid the solar anger. It would be a long, hot walk, but it always feels even longer than you expect, especially after being on the hills right through the night. We were marching on, but we had that weariness of the final lap which means no one is talking. There's just a grim determination to conserve as much energy, as much strength, as possible.

Pauline tried to lift the spirits: "This is just like running a marathon."

James pointed out: "Except if this was a marathon, we would have been finished eight hours ago."

He had a point. The silence resumed.

The car park never seemed to be getting any closer, the track stretching on to the horizon, and then it was there, a cut through the trees that we had failed to notice. Now a nap was possible. I moved my car over to the shadier side and sprawled out on the passenger seat, while the others resumed their positions in the van with the doors wide open. Ninety minutes later, we were on the road again. We had a long drive over to Corran to join up with the rest of the club for another three days' walking.

We lasted all of 20 minutes in the oppressive heat. As soon as we reached Cannich, it was into the village store and ice cream bars and bottles of fizzy juice all round. This didn't count as a meal, so we stopped again at Spean Bridge for a second, or maybe third, lunch. Gourmet was out, stodge the order of the day. James and I ordered the chicken curry.

The waitress asked: "Do you want that with rice or chips?"

We weren't expecting the Spean Bridge Inquisition. I mean, who asks tricky questions like that? Could she not see we were barely conscious?

And then, before we could make a choice, she added: "Or

do you want both?" Now she was an angel rather than a tease.

Refreshed, we made it to Corran. We got our rooms sorted out, showered, and then took the ferry over the Narrows to the pub for whatever meal we were at now. Japan and Poland were kicking lumps out of each other on the box. Or maybe it was Senegal and Colombia. The countries, like the days, all seemed to be rolling into one. Sleep came easy, with the comforting thought that breakfast wasn't too far away.

Pauline and I opted for an easier next day, a shorter climb up through the butterfly reserve on the shores of Loch Arkaig, while James went for the two Munros at Mile Dorcha. We thought he was pushing it too much in the heat, and unfortunately we were proven right. He left his sunscreen behind and then quickly ran out of fluid and had to bale after the first ascent. Our initial ascent was more pleasant but then we ran into a painful infestation of horseflies. Midges are bad, but clegs are worse. They were everywhere; the only way to escape was to keep going higher.

The heat was playing havoc with the natural order; at one point we saw a vole and a toad crossing the road in opposite directions, passing each other without a sideways glance.

We met back at the falls at Mile Dorcha and went swimming under the waterfall. A few hours later, I looked as if I had measles. The top half of my body was covered in angry red spots. I hadn't noticed any midges, so I had to assume they were cleg bites.

The strength and longevity of the heatwave were driven home when I travelled round to Moidart the next day. Glen Moidart is said to be the wettest in the country, yet I trod the full circuit without getting my boots wet. Another three-course dinner and then I managed a final weary day from Strontian. It was time to go for a rest – and a slap-up meal, of course.

8
Passing the Buck

BUCK MOON

(Friday, July 27, 21.20)
Mountain: *Gleouraich, Spidean Mialach*
Soundtrack: *Boulevard of Broken Dreams – Green Day*
Celebratory drink: *Stag Beer*

I had been lucky to have been granted three perfect full moon walks in a row but the Buck Moon promised to be the most exciting yet.

The eighth full moon of the year was due to coincide with the longest lunar eclipse of the century. This also made it a blood moon, so-called because the moon appears to glow a rusty red during the eclipse as it passes across the Earth's shadow and its brightness starts to fade.

All fine and well if you are living in the Middle East. The chances of seeing this spectacular show from Scotland were not so good. With this in mind, I decided to hedge my bets and try to go out twice in the same 24 hours.

The Algonquian called this the Buck Moon as young stags'

antlers are in full growth. It is also common to hear it referred to as the Thunder Moon, because of the increased likelihood of thunderstorms at this time of year. It seems I wasn't the only one hedging my bets.

Other epithets are Hay Moon, an old Anglo-Saxon reference to the hay harvest that took place during this month, or Wort Moon, as July was the time to gather herbs to use as spices and remedies. But the prize for the best name of all goes to the Chinese. They call this the Hungry Ghost Moon, a time when spirits roam the Earth searching for something to feed on. In a bid to satisfy those needs and pacify the spirits, the living offer gifts of food and charms. It seems to work. Who knows? Maybe if the exorcist had just turned up with a good helping of steak pie, all that head-spinning nonsense and vulgar insults could have been avoided. Vegan options are available.

I have to admit to a personal preference for Thunder. It conjures up a more realistic picture of a Scottish summer of instant monsoons, the rain starting and stopping at the flick of a switch like a power shower, while the thunderous bellows of the gods' royal rumble plays out overhead. But rules are rules, so despite its more American sounding name, I went with the Buck.

There was no shortage of candidates for the walk; the number of Scottish mountains whose names are connected to deer are widespread. There's Stob Diamh, 'peak of the stag', in the Cruachan range, which is also home to the Corbett, Beinn a' Bhuiridh, 'hill of bellowing (of stags)'. There's the similarly named Meall a' Bhuiridh rising above the western edge of Rannoch Moor. Ben Wyvis was also a possibility, with its prominent frontal top of An Cabar, 'the antler'. There were also Munros whose names referred to hinds, Beinn nan Aighenan in Glen Etive, and Sgurr Eilde Mor in the Mamores. For the real treasure trove, there was only one place. The mountains which rise from the sides of Loch Quoich along the single-track road to Kinloch Hourn reflect the prevalence and importance of deer to this area. There's Gleouraich, which means 'roaring', and its partner, Spidean Mialach, 'peak of the deer'. Across the water is the graceful Gairich, another hill whose name evokes the bellowing of stags.

The other determining factor was that the short circuit of Gleouraich and Spidean Mialach was one of the first night walks I had done back in 1995. We were in the midst of a long, hot spell, and I drove a lot of the way with the windows cracked open to catch the welcome breeze. The final approach along this glen was shrouded in ground-hugging mist, and when I set off on the stalker's path through the thick rhododendron bushes, visibility was limited to a few feet. I soon emerged from the mist, but it was still stubbornly clinging to floor of the glen, hiding the waters of the loch.

The view from the beehive cairn on Gleouraich at 4.30am was across a vast sea of cotton wool with just the islands of the higher mountains piercing the surface, the walk on to Spidean Mialach through a waterfall of rolling cloud, which tumbled across the bealach with a hypnotically lazy flow. The heat at the second summit was intense, the descent back into the cloud accompanied by a Brocken Spectre of alien features. The mist seemed to sink with me, and by the time I was back at the car the day had evolved into wall to wall sunshine, perfect for a casual return journey. It would be good to revisit the scene of one of the most memorable night ascents.

I have had a few interesting encounters with deer in this glen. On an October ascent of Sgurr a' Mhaoraich, bang in the middle of the rutting season, I came across a belligerent stag standing his ground. It was somewhat ironic that he had claimed the stalker's path as his own but he was in no mood to budge and I took a wide detour to avoid upsetting him further.

I had flashbacks to this encounter during another ascent of this peak. Late November and I was crawling along on the ice-sheathed road when I noticed a stag standing close enough for a picture opportunity. I stopped the car, but he made no attempt to run. Then I became aware of two more cautiously coming round the other side of the car. I thought: Ambush. I edged back into the vehicle and carried on to my starting point. As I was getting changed, another stag appeared, then another. A few minutes later, and there were at least half a dozen surrounding the car, but keeping a safe distance of a few feet away. I was wary, but none made any further move, and I eventually set off up the path without being followed. I later learned they were waiting for food. The rut was over and they were fresh out of testosterone. The fight had left them, along with some 20 per cent of their body fat. A month of shouting, fighting and the other thing will do that. Now their focus was on getting fattened up again before the winter snows arrived. Every day, an estate vehicle would drive along this road dispersing food and they had simply mistaken my car for the chuck wagon.

After three walks with company, I was reverting to going solo. The settled conditions we had enjoyed for so long had finally broken and the unpredictability of the weather meant the logistics of trying to liaise with anyone at short notice would be awkward. I wanted to be able to change my plans at the last second without any great fuss, so it seemed easier to go it alone.

The timing of the full moon – it fell at 21.20 on the Friday evening – gave me the scope of going out any hour that day. I just had to be out with the moon on the 27th, even if it only involved a few minutes of that date. I was due to meet a group at Aultguish for the weekend, so there was no time pressure. No one would be wondering where I had got to. My time was my own, and I was going to chase the best conditions I could find.

§

I HAVE been night walking for some 25 years, the majority solo. So while the choice of Green Day's Boulevard of Broken Dreams as the soundtrack for the walk may seem a little odd, there is method in the supposed madness. There's no reference to the moon or stags in the lyrics, but the constant refrain of 'I Walk Alone' was one that had been going round in my head for many years. This was an earworm song for me, and on a night with a full moon, alone on the ascent of a hill, the line, 'My shadow's the only one that walks beside me' seemed to fit the moment. It's always there alongside me. Not much of a conversationalist, but a good listener. Besides, I like the silence.

Music has always played a huge part in my mountain life. All those nights alone on the road to faraway places, a long-running festival of eclectic tracks to rival the shows of Bob Harris or Iain Anderson. A typical journey would start with the whispered tones of a late-night radio offering, then a switch to my own collection when the reception faded away.

I had always been into a wide variety of sounds, but 15 years of regular three and four-hour trips after midnight allowed me to sample so much I would otherwise have missed. Most of us have songs that define who we are. When I played football, every match had its own song. When played now they invoke pictures of a certain day, a certain era. Memories long forgotten suddenly resurface with the first notes.

The emotional impact should never be underestimated. I have often found an extra spring in my ascent of a mountain slope with Dougie MacLean's The Gael playing out in my head. Its power is immeasurable. Just as I want my ashes scattered on Buachaille Etive Mor, I want The Gael to be the accompaniment to my funeral march. Listen carefully – you may hear me humming along from inside the box.

The mood of the music can change dramatically with the journey. I used to find that gentler sounds were the best for the dark hours, John Martyn or Southside Johnnie and the Ashbury Dukes for instance, every little hiss and silence feeding perfectly into each mile.

If it was raining heavily then the percussion on the car roof could be complemented by Michael Chapman's *Rainmaker*, if the light was coming up and the travelling smooth then there was a lot of mileage in Little Feat. But often the last 20 minutes before arrival saw a switch to something heavy, an awakening from the mellow mood, Led Zeppelin or Deep Purple to get the juices flowing and the psyche engaged for the task ahead. It may sound obvious, but Run DMC's Walk This Way was another favourite in the build-up.

This rock and awe treatment worked a treat over the years. I got out of the car with an adrenaline rush already in place – and Green Day were major contributors.

It was a tactic I eventually employed to great effect on others. There were eight of us in Skye – Cuillin the Gang, if you like – and I was the only one who had climbed all the peaks on the ridge. For the rest this was virgin territory, and there were a lot of shaky legs with the thought of what lay ahead.

We were staying at Sligachan and it was a 20-minute run down to our starting point each day. On the first day, I put on the wildest, noisiest tracks from Green Day's *American*

Idiot. It worked. Everyone arrived pumped up and ready to go. It became the soundtrack for the week, and everyone got their Munros ticked. It was the week everyone was a rock star.

With the latest incumbent in the White House creating bemusement on a daily basis, I suspect *American Idiot* will getting more airplay than ever before.

When it came to finding a suitable drink, again I was spoilt for choice; there are many, many beers and lagers with stag in the name or in the logo. One left-field suggestion came from a friend in Glasgow.

"Buck Moon? It's got to be a bottle of Buckie then."

It was hard to argue with the logic, but necking a bottle of cheap, fortified wine to celebrate a mountain walk would be like turning up at a funeral in a clown costume. It only works if you are there to see Bozo off on his final journey. Buckfast as a hillwalker's tipple? We have enough to worry about with the increasing industrial vandalism being perpetrated on our wild places and the explosion of litter without having to step over vomit-stained drunks in technical jackets and Scarpa-shod beggars behind every boulder asking if you could spare 50p for a Soreen loaf.

§

I SPENT a few days watching the weather, then decided to go early. The forecast was for a fine evening which would hold until after midnight, cloud building through the night, the grey then threatening to spill its tears the next day.

The evening sky was a flawless deep blue, the dark sentinels of the Commando Memorial at Spean Bridge gazing over at the unsullied peaks of the Nevis Range and the Grey Corries. Onward: The merest pirr on the waters of Loch Lochy, a glint of sun from the top of Ben Tee, a dapple of light through the lush, green guard of honour on the road past Tomdoun.

I was greeted by a wonderful sunset as I drove along the lochside, the western skies luminescent, huge, flocculent, spaceship clouds hanging in suspended animation, a vast array of mountains forming a dark, jagged outline in a horseshoe round the head of the loch. Sgurr na Ciche, rough and remote, the mini-Matterhorn of the region, took centre stage, flanked on the left by the bulky yet elegant Sgurr Mor, and on the right by Ben Aden. Beyond lay the big boys of Knoydart, their scale vastly reduced, a sobering reminder of the long walk in.

I stopped at a favourite lochside spot and watched the moon rise and strengthen over Gairich. I still had three hours until midnight. I decided to drive further along to the bridge and take in the views from there. What I saw nearly brought me to tears of sadness and rage. Here was another example of industrial vandalism; a track bulldozed up the left side of the inlet leading into Glen Quoich for hydro work, no subtlety, no attempt to mitigate the damage. The glen had a scar the width of a major road, complete with collapsed edges and rubble shoved off in heaps to the sides.

I tried to ignore the abomination and turned back to Gairich to watch the moon's progress. Its brightness was increasing in tandem with the darkening of the landscape, with a sprinkling of stars providing support. The disordered cirque of mountains was now dark blue, the waters below several shades lighter, the moon's silver sheen a ragged sheet elongated on the water.

I returned to the walk starting point and settled down to wait for midnight and the turn into a new day which would signal the green light. I thought I might manage to grab a couple of hours shuteye but the brilliance of the moon through the windscreen was like a searchlight. I reckoned if I stared hard enough I might be able to make out Neil Armstrong's footprints. It seemed omnipotent, huge and overpowering, yet this was the most distant and smallest full moon of the year, more than 250,000 miles away. In Munro money, that's around 156 rounds. The moon is said to be drifting away from us, slowly but surely, at a rate of four centimetres per year, just one more reason why I was glad I had made the effort this year.

It seemed incredible to think it had been nearly 50 years since we were gathered round the old black and white telly to watch grainy pictures being beamed back to Earth of the Apollo 11 mission and man's first steps on the moon. Sunday, July 20, 1969, and our view from Earth had been of a slim crescent moon. This was the moon in a waxing crescent phase, the first phase after the new moon. As a child, I looked up in awe – how had they had managed to land on such a slim target? These guys must have been good.

There's no shortage of conspiracy theories about whether it was all faked. One of the recurring themes is that the tread on Armstrong's boots didn't match the prints on the surface, but this is easily swept aside. He was wearing overshoes for his walk, which were then left behind. It's easily done. Coincidentally, and rather spookily, I once left behind a pair of boots in the farmhouse at the end of this road. Close encounters, indeed. It's also suggested that the prints famously pictured may have been those made by the second man, Buzz Aldrin, rather than Armstrong. Having seen Aldrin's right hook to the jaw of a disbeliever, I've decided it's safer to keep the faith.

Only 12 people have walked on the moon, all male and all American, the last being Gene Cernan in 1972. At the height of the Cold War, the Americans considered carrying out a nuclear explosion on the moon as a show of strength to make up for lagging behind the Russians in the space race.

If you can't beat 'em, bomb 'em. Recently, the Chinese landed a robotic spacecraft on the surface. They planted seeds of cotton, potato and rapeseed but the plants withered and died in the bitter cold of the long lunar nights. They may also have sown the seeds of a new space race. Let's hope the Americans don't feel too miffed in this one.

It feels as though it's only matter of time before human colonies are set up on the moon, but there are still huge hurdles to overcome. The moon has no atmosphere but then that's never stopped Coldplay performing. It does mean that the surface has no protection from cosmic rays, meteorites and solar winds, and there are huge temperature variations. It also suffers from regular quakes.

If there's the slightest possibility of money to be made, the superpowers will continue striving to set up house. The fact that weaker gravity means a person weighs less on the moon is a gilt-edged opportunity for anyone with a slimming franchise. No need to bother with any diets or exercise, just book a ticket to the moon and five-sixths of your body weight becomes irrelevant. You can bounce around all day without a care in the (new) world. Give it 50 years, and I'm also sure there will be Munro baggers clamouring to do the ultimate Three Peaks challenge in their Rab and Berghaus branded spacesuits.

§

FIFTEEN minutes before my launch time, and I was geared to go. The clock struck the magic hour and I left the car to be a greeted by the invisible menace – midges. This was my first real taste of the little darlings on these walks, and it appeared that they had set up a summer jamboree to welcome me back. The one advantage of a plague of the wee beasties is that they focus the mind on the task ahead. There's no hanging about; you are off on the incline as fast as you go, hands swatting frantically yet ultimately helplessly until you have outrun the initial assault.

The stalker's path up Gleouraich is one of the finest in the country and makes for fast progress even in the dark, perfectly cut lengthy zig-zags in its infancy and then a high-level route which pushes out to the edge of the slope above the small inlaid section of the loch before the final, steeper climb through the clink and clatter of rocks underfoot to the huge cairn.

The contrast to my last night visit here couldn't have been starker. Then I had risen with the sunrise, the mist sticking closely behind like a faithful mutt following its master. I was welcomed to the summit by an ocean of cloud as far as the eye could see with flawless skies above and every peak for some 50 miles in every direction sparkling and reflecting rainbow beams. This time, the cairn seemed parked in a void, darkness swallowing all the views, all sense of distance and depth absent. The night vision camera picked up every stone on the cairn, every vein, every striation, every glint of mineral deposit, and every shining blade of grass. Beyond that lay a black emptiness, a bottomless pit. Spidean Mialach was just over three kilometres off to the east, but I only had the evidence of the map for that.

The moon was glowing yellow now but its light had severely diminished since my rise from the loch and the next section needed some careful foot picking through slippery rocks, the thin coating of moisture picked up by the beam of my head torch. Navigation was simple, a continuing curving line with the benefit of a handrail along the ridge line always on my left, but otherwise there were precious little clues to the lie of the land.

As I dropped off the back of an intervening top, Creag Coire na Fiar Bhealaich, I caught the first hint of fresh light, a burnt orange glow off to the north. Bubbled cloud stood over this fiery horizon, the canvas topped by a pale, bluish-grey wash. As I descended to the bealach on the twisting path, the moon was being absorbed by the cloud. Then what little remained disappeared altogether, cut off by the dark slopes behind me. The terrain ahead was still hidden, a surprise yet to be unveiled. I dropped my pack for a drink and a quick bite. By the time I had lifted it again, Spidean Mialach had emerged from the liquid night, a mountain mirage. The first flash of morning had been fired. There was no stopping it now. I was reinvigorated by the sight of this old friend towering out of the gloom.

The walk to the summit was over more false rises and falls than the memory had stored, but that's the nature of walking at this time of the morning. The dominating colour was blue. The sky was layered from azure white, through powder, then Columbia into Carolina, the mountain lines below increasing in depth of shade with every step forward from the far horizon, the blue remembered hills of A.E. Housman brought to mind. Even the tumbled rocks on the slopes were tinged with blue. The only concession came from the occasional vertical stripes of green, but even the vegetation appeared to be swithering in its loyalty. It left the view from the untidy spill of rocks which marked the summit muted. It didn't help that the initial emergence of sunrise was blocked by towering cloud, a portent of the weather to come. The overall effect was massively underwhelming, a disappointment after the fireworks of sunset.

It improved on the descent west, Gairich again coming to the rescue, leading the line of glowing copper mountains to the head of the loch. Gleouraich was catching what little sun there was on its eastern face as I dropped in the shadow of the ridge.

Then, a warning bark cut through the air; a female deer and its offspring, perfectly camouflaged in the low morning light, suddenly up and running just a few hundred metres away. It suddenly struck me that had been what was missing – the wildlife had been conspicuous by its absence during the last 12 hours or so. There was no birdsong, no darting rabbits or hares, no deer so far, only the midges and the plentiful droppings of the cattle which grazed along the side of this road.

I turned to look back at the peak I had just descended. There were hundreds of deer. The slopes of Coire Glas were teeming with them. I hadn't managed to catch sight of a young buck by moonlight, but this was the consolation, several of them in plain sight, antlers glowing silver with the sunlight flashing off velvet. A couple of months from now and they would be readying for combat, their head gear fully formed, machismo on full show.

I continued to drop on the diagonal above the hanging Loch Fearna to pick up the path down the final stretch. Inevitably I came across another messily bulldozed track, another run of river scheme, which led to the road. I reached the car at 7am in need of a nap. The rest of the world didn't seem to have wakened yet, and I drove along the road to my refuge and settled down in the passenger seat with Gairich watching over me. Two and a half hours later I woke, ready for part two of the night adventure and hopefully a date with the longest total lunar eclipse in roughly 100 years.

There are two types of eclipse – solar and lunar. During a solar eclipse, the moon passes between Earth and the sun to cast its shadow on our planet, but the shadow is colourless because the moon has no atmosphere to scatter or refract any sunlight. During a lunar eclipse, the Earth passes between the moon and the sun casting a shadow on the moon. Earth's atmosphere is filled with nitrogen which takes in white sunlight and a mix of colours. It scatters around the blues which gives our sky its colour. Around sunset and sunrise, the light becomes more scattered. We lose nearly all the blue and instead have a sun that appears a deeper orange or even red. In a lunar eclipse, the Earth acts like a gigantic lens, refracting that light toward the moon. It then bounces off the surface of the moon creating a blood-orange glow, hence the term blood moon.

The total lunar eclipse would last one hour and 43 minutes, four minutes short of the longest possible. With moonrise at 21.20 in Scotland, it was hoped we would be able to see at least part of the eclipse. There was even the possibility of seeing a brighter than usual Mars complementing the blood moon. Two for the price of one. Then the rider, two words that resonate with every person north of the border: weather dependent. In other words, nae chance.

I drove to Aultguish, checked in, showered and had a meal, and then, with that peculiarly unique Scottish blend of pessimism and optimism, set off back to Achnasheen in deteriorating conditions to wait for any sign of the blood moon.

Achnasheen means 'field of the storms' and it seemed a perfect setting for the Thunder Moon. I thought I could do a double-header and climb Fionn Bheinn, which sits above the village, to encompass both the Buck and Thunder variations of this moon. Two for the price of one. At the very least, I hoped for the consolation of a glimpse of red across the loch. Better still, accompanied by a thunderstorm of biblical proportions. I got neither. It stayed grey and threatening, no moon, no light. I sat in the car at the side of the loch terrified to move off in case the cloud parted for one millisecond and I missed the night show. It was only when the time crept past 10.30, I felt satisfied that I had made every effort to roll as much as I could into one long day.

When I returned to the base at Aultguish, I was informed that the blood moon had been particularly vibrant in Lebanon. Thanks for that. My decision to go earlier had been vindicated.

9

Two Men in a Boat

STURGEON MOON

(Sunday, August 26, 12.56)
Mountain: *Ben Starav*
Soundtrack: *Fish Rising – Steve Hillage*
Celebratory drink: *Kelpie Seaweed Beer*

Our destination for late August was big, bold Ben Starav but for once this night walk was not all about the mountain. This was the time of year when the rivers and lakes were teeming with fish and the catches bountiful, so it was fitting the chosen hill should be approached from the water. Ben Starav's domineering position ticked all the boxes. It's one of few Munros that can be accessed directly from the waterside, slopes sweeping straight up from the eastern shores of Loch Etive. I can't take credit for the idea, though.

The plan was hatched, as most good ones are, over a few drinks during a late-night session in a pub. I was in Aviemore as one of a panel of outdoor speakers for a Bookweek Scotland event. It was the first time I had talked about my Mountains of the Moon ambitions. The schedule was still a work in progress and there were some notable gaps, including the one for the Sturgeon Moon.

One of my fellow panellists was Patrick Baker, author of *The Secret History of the Cairngorms*, and a lover of the hidden corners of our landscape. Patrick's imagination had been whetted by my plans and he was keen to join me for a night out. We retired to the bar to discuss. I had been kicking around a few ideas about mountains with direct links to water or fish but it was all fairly vague. I had spotted Meall an Iasgaich, 'hill of the sturgeon', on South Uist, but it was a minor protuberance, merely a few hundred feet high. It would have to have been something special to make me consider bending my Munros rule. Besides, the logistics of reaching this remote little island peak and then the prospect of having to traverse tough heather-cloaked rises riddled with hidden, ankle-breaking holes in the dark didn't appeal.

There's Loch an Iasgaich on Skye, but I already had my target for the Misty Isle, Bla Bheinn, for the Blue Moon in late March. Then there were mountain names that referenced shellfish – Sgurr a' Mhaoraich at the head of Loch Hourn, whose slopes are covered in fragments of crustacean shells dropped by birds feasting in the loch – or creels – A' Chralaig in Glen Shiel – although that has more to do with the shape of the mountain than any direct fishing link.

I turned to myths and monsters but there's a lack of Munros along the shores of Loch Ness and Loch Monar, the domains of Nessie and Morag respectively. Virtually every body of water in the country has legends of kelpies. One of the most famous tales of these mythical water horses surrounds Beinn Alligin, a mountain already set aside for the Wolf Moon.

The only mythological creature associated with Glen Etive

seemed to be the fachan, a malevolent. furry giant with just one leg, a single hand emanating from the centre of its body in place of arms, and one eye in the centre of the head. It was also follically challenged, just a tuft of black hair or sometimes feathers. It was said to wield a spiked club and would destroy anything or anyone that crossed its path. There was no clue as to its attitude to fish.

I needed something more precise, more focused. That's where Patrick came in. He suggested finding a mountain that could be directly accessed from the water. This had the added attraction of approaching by canoe, a nod to the common method of transport used by the tribes who had inspired this whole undertaking. We shook on it and agreed to meet nine months later.

Now here we were at the head of Loch Etive, in the midge-infested stillness of a Saturday evening, hauling Patrick's canoe down to the shore. The weeks since the Buck Moon walk had been a typical Scottish summer mix; warm and claggy, wet and windy, punctuated by the odd clear day. This had produced another anxious watch; the conditions had to be decent to go out on the loch. Patrick was an experienced canoeist but I wasn't. We needed a calm spell on the water. I would be climbing Ben Starav no matter what, but it would have been devastating after months of anticipation if we had to forgo the canoe and see this moon walk relegated to a drearily ordinary night walking round indistinguishable bumps.

If I was looking for signs of optimism, the astrological charts handily pointed out that this full moon would be in Pisces. This zodiac sign is said to allow you to swim deep through the waters of your unconscious. I didn't like the sound of that. Swimming and unconsciousness are two things I specifically hoped to avoid while paddling across a deep loch. I decided I would be as well putting one of those red cellophane fish in the palm of my hand and see which way it curled.

I had experienced first-hand the perils of water crossings. I had been on the fast boat from Mallaig to Knoydart with two friends, a last-minute decision to go for an ascent of Luinne Bheinn, a big, bold and beautiful peak at the head of the Mam Barrisdale pass. It is often affectionately referred to Loony Bin. You could say it was appropriate on this occasion. For three supposedly clued-up mountaineers, we produced a catalogue of errors.

The night before our trip, my friends volunteered to give me a day off by doing the navigation. That was the first mistake. As they couldn't find the required map at such short notice, I handed them mine to do the calculations. That was my second mistake: never part company with your map.

They had it worked out, every step, every co-ordinate, every twist in the route. They showed me their calculations. Mistake No.3. They had planned a route up Meall Buidhe, a nice hill but not the one we were aiming for.

Armed with just one map between three of us – biggest mistake yet, you should always have a map of your own, or at worst two between three – we boarded the boat. And this was where the mother and father of all cock-ups happened.

As we sat waiting for the boat to leave the harbour, one friend took the map out of her rucksack to recheck her calculations. Satisfied she had cracked it, she put the map down on the seat beside her with her rucksack on top. As we got further out in the water and picked up speed, the swell also started picking up. My map-reading pal was leaning over taking a picture when she was soaked by the incoming spray. Her automatic reaction was to jump back and grab her rucksack to save it getting wet. She forgot the map was underneath. Another lesson: when on a fast-moving boat always make sure your map is inside your rucksack or at least securely clipped on to something. Before anyone could yell map overboard, the map was, well, overboard.

We survived Luinne Bheinn. Had the weather been bad, we would have abandoned the walk. But we managed to get up and down again without any mishap.

For the boat trip back, I had suggested tying a rope to my friend and heaving her over the side so she could dredge the waters looking for the map as we retraced our passage to Mallaig. I would like to report a happier ending, like a Flipper wannabe swimming up to the boat having found my map or simply that it had floated back into the harbour, but it wasn't to be. If you are ever walking up Luinne Bheinn and are passed by a group of Faroese fishermen, you'll know where my map finally washed up.

§

THE moon walks so far had thrown up one curious fact: I hadn't encountered rain. I had walked in blizzards, but not one drop of rain. When I started out, I had fully expected some long, wet nights. Precipitation is a simply a fact of life here. But happy as I was with this state of affairs, I was also becoming very nervous. A good soaking was overdue.

Not that there was any shortage of rain through August. Two days in Glen Shiel at the start of the month had more than made up for the summer drought. We left Beauly under a beautiful sunrise, but as we headed west, the skies had taken on a more ominous complexion. The seven Munros of the South Shiel Ridge were buried in dark fluff, swirling and sliding along and between the contours, as we made our made up the old military road to the start of our ascent.

Despite the forecast, we retained that sense of impossible optimism that hillwalkers show against all odds. We could now almost see the top part of the first mountain, the slopes sweeping ahead vibrant green and purple. We dared to think we might get away with it. As the cloud continued to pile up in every direction, we were treated to a burst of brilliance through the gloom turning the entire length of Loch Cluanie sparkling silver. It was only 9am, but it turned out this was the sun saying goodbye for the rest of the day: You're on your own now, boys.

It was obvious the damp weather had been no stranger to these slopes in the previous few days. The path was a quagmire, boots submerged with every squelching step. Then it started raining. It was easy to go off path; the water pouring downhill was concealing the true way ahead.

I don't mind walking in the rain. I don't dance with joy with the idea of trudging round in torrential conditions. But there is something almost therapeutic about walking in the rain, something akin to a cleansing of the body and soul. Not everyone agrees. Some of my fellow walkers make Goldilocks seem positively agreeable. They moan when the weather is wet, yet they moan when it is dry and hot. They moan when it's windy and when there is no breeze. This is Scotland. It rains. Get over it.

If you are properly geared up then wet weather can produce some of the best mountain experiences. Those days when the mists keep a lot of the treasures hidden for so long before clearing just enough to give you a glimpse of something special; wet rocks and slabs glistening in the newly victorious light, waterfalls pouring down every gully, from every crevice. It's a triumph of light over darkness, the terrain and the air cleansed and reset.

The slow reveal is always far more rewarding than having

the whole picture in front of you for hours on end. That's probably why my idea for a strip club which reversed the process never caught on. No one wants to watch a naked person getting dressed.

During regular weekly walks in years gone by, we used to pick the day with the best weather prospects. But it was one day when the forecast went awry that turned out to be one of the finest. Instead of the expected sunshine and clear skies, we had shifting mist and dampness. When the conditions cleared and we saw the until-then hidden slopes of Beinn Ime towering above us, you could hear the collective sound of awe. This was truly magnificent.

I can't say I was overjoyed to see the heavens open on this occasion, but at least it was warm, and we were moving fast enough to outfox the midges. Our arrival at the summit cairn of Creag a' Mhaim didn't produce any views but it did produce an opportunity to give our feet a helping hand. We took off our boots and tipped out the contents of Lake Scarpa, grateful we had been wise enough to pull on waterproof socks that morning. The walk across the other six summits and down the higher part of corrie was mostly blind, but apart from one stretch of thundering water to wade through, it was all quite leisurely. It helped that we had the foresight to leave a car at the finish point to save a seven-mile trudge back up the road. The chances of two extremely soggy gents getting a lift, even in this hitchhiking hotspot, would have been remote. We went for the wet and windy experience again the next day, on the Five Sisters ridge across the glen. This time our optimism did pay off, and about halfway round the cloud lifted and the rain ceased.

The unpredictability continued. I arrived at Lochgoilhead for a sunshine circuit only to be greeted by torrential downpours. Stunned holidaymakers were walking round in tee-shirts, shorts and ponchos, the water cascading over their flip-flops. This change of fortune was confusing: which gear to wear? It felt as though lightweight could lead to hypothermia, but it was too warm to layer up. The rain had subsided by the time I made a decision but the ground was saturated. By the time I had fought my way through the dripping long grass and deep, vegetated cover, I was left with a curious problem. My top half was overheating, while my legs and feet were freezing with the sheer volume of water that had found its way in. My core was confused. I had no strength. I had to stop for a breather every couple of minutes. It took me nearly seven hours to get round these two smaller hills, only an hour less than it took to do seven Munros a few days earlier.

The new moon was at perigree – the closest point to Earth, a moon at apogee is at the furthest point – which made it a supermoon, but as the new moon is invisible to us, it slipped by unnoticed. The following week I was pining for the cool, fresh rain during a family visit to London. The week seemed to be divided between travelling around in the high-speed sardine tins they call the Underground, and trying to win a staring contest with the black mambas at the zoo. I'm not a fan of zoos, but I am fascinated by snakes, especially the more exotic varieties, and this is probably the only place I will ever be able to see the deadly mamba at close range. I love the graceful way they move, how they control every single muscle while on the move, and how they manage to look permanently angry. That last one is probably down to the hassles of the daily commute. A week in any big city is always a trigger for an immediate return to the great outdoors and I was itching to get into that canoe. I still had a few days to kill though, and I spent them concentrating on my choice of alcohol and music.

Fish-themed labelling was not providing too many candidates, but then technically I could have chosen from the hundreds of beers which include isinglass, a gelatine made from fish bladders. This odourless ingredient has been used by many brewers for years to make beer clear, bright and more attractive to drinkers who didn't fancy a cloudy pint. Those who talk about getting bladdered probably don't realise how accurate they are. There would have been no such problems in the USA. They have countless beers with fish motifs with some wonderfully bonkers names such as Mouthy Muskie, Stump Knocker and my favourite, Mouthin' Crappie. There is also a Canadian beer called Cracked Canoe but I reckoned that would be a bad omen.

When it came to the musical accompaniment, I deferred to my music guru friend Frank who can come up with a song for every occasion. In this case, he reminded me of an album I liked back in my guitar hero times, when all was long hair and loon pants. *Fish Rising* by Steve Hillage also includes The Salmon Song. Now we were getting somewhere.

§

PATRICK was catching forty winks when I arrived in Tyndrum late on the Saturday afternoon. Just as the canoe trip to climb a Munro would be a new experience for me, the night climb was a first for him. He was getting his retaliatory sleep in first. It was warm and muggy as we travelled down the length of Glen Etive on the winding single track road which runs for twelve and a half miles to the head of the sea loch.

Both sides of the road were dotted with bright colours, the camping fraternity out in force. It's an area that has had its problems over recent years with an unsavoury element who think it's their right to leave behind their smouldering camp fires, empty cans and bottles and trashed gear for someone else to pick up. It all looked peaceful so far, a lot of families enjoying the great outdoors. The acid test would come when everyone had packed up and left.

The full moon was due at 56 minutes past midnight, but we couldn't wait until then. We had to cross the loch during the remaining daylight hours, walk through the night into a new day, and then be ready to come back over the water when the light had returned. We didn't want to be on the water in darkness.

We managed to squeeze in to the parking area at Gualachulain, the smell of barbecue permeating the evening air. There was no escaping the midges. We went down to the shore to look for a good launch point, and already they were gathering. We now had to spend 20 minutes fending them off while we unhooked the canoe and then carried it down to the waterside.

The loch resembled a sheet of glass. The spiked ridge of the Ben Cruachan range held the centre view miles away in the distance, the uprooted skeleton of a tree providing the foreground to the deep V between Buachailles to the north. But the eyes were mainly drawn to Ben Starav rising unhindered along the length of the eastern shore, its slopes pale green in the evening light, interrupted only by ragged, rocky, grey gullies spilling down its mighty facade.

Still swatting the midges, we slipped into the water, no owl, no pussycat, just a beautiful pea green boat (marrowfat rather than garden, I would say) and cautiously edged round the waving grasses and hidden ledges of the shallows before turning left to make a direct crossing towards the eastern shore. Patrick was on the bow seat, I was on the stern. The rucksacks were stored in the wide centre of the hull under the yoke, along with the dry sacks. We passed a young couple coming towards us, neither of them wearing life preservers, although there was no denying they seemed to know what they were doing. We made fast progress for the half kilometre or so across the centre of the loch, cutting through the still water with ease, no wind resistance. The mountain seemed to rear higher over us with every stroke. Patrick kept us on course, telling me when and how hard to paddle every time he spotted the potential for trouble, the only sounds breaking the silence of the evening. Close your eyes, and you could imagine paddling down one of the mighty American or Canadian lakes with a pile of pelts as cargo.

Three kilometres further on and we were hauling the canoe ashore over the pebbles and rough grass at Rubha Doire Larach. We had made good time but the difference in the light was already noticeable. The night was starting to assert itself. The forecast was for a generally clear evening with cloud building into the early hours and rain driving in behind. We wanted to get round the mountain and back over the loch before things started going downhill.

We secured the canoe then climbed through rough terrain to reach the Allt Coire na Larach, the stream that tumbles down the steep corrie which divides the main bulk of the mountain from the walls of the Stob an Duine Ruaidh ridge. Ben Starav is a popular hill, but most walkers approach it from Coileitir and the stepped north-east ridge. We were coming in from the back, climbing the pathless south-west ridge. This is the hidden side of the mountain, one for the purist.

I have circuited Starav once before. We came in the trade route on a day of low cloud and drizzle then left the few other walkers in the mist at the summit cairn to head south to the top of Meall Cruidh. We continued to follow the ridge amongst the outcrops and pavement slabs as it swung round to the final peak of Stob an Duine Ruaidh. It was a steep and cautious drop through the crags to the rubble and stream far below. The cloud had lifted and the sun was out, but it still felt a long trek along the loch. My companion that day remembers the descent and walk out as one of the roughest he's had to endure.

The distance from shore to summit is just over three kilometres, but it gives little respite from sea level until the 900-metre contour is reached, a constantly steep push, first through deep grass then scree and boulder stretches. It was often a case of two steps forward, one step back for Patrick and myself on almost vertiginous muddy ledges which had a habit of collapsing as soon as a boot hit them. The angle of the climb made the stream seem a long way down. The slickness and steepness of the ground made one decision easy: we would not be descending this way. Coming off this ground in the dark would not be a safe option. We would make the complete circuit, over the summit and down the more stable north-east ridge.

The peaks on the southern horizon were being rapidly swallowed by cloud as we rose, the light fading with the views. As yet, there was no sign of the moon. About halfway up, the rain came on and we feared the weather had made an early power grab. The waterproofs went on and the head torches came out, but a few minutes later clarity was restored; it was still dark but that short burst of rain seemed to have cleared the air and the varieties and shades of green under the torchlight were emboldened.

We caught the glow on the ridge line to the east. Another few metres of ascent and we could see the Sturgeon Moon, a penumbral ball of fuzz, as though in need of fine tuning. Seconds later, it was gone. We continued to catch glimpses throughout the next few hours amongst the dark shadows of the skyline. It seemed to be swimming beneath the surface of a sea of cloud, occasionally cresting before diving back beneath the billowing waves.

We reached what we thought was the breakthrough point, cresting one rise to see the summit cairn at the apex of three fine ridges silhouetted on the skyline ahead. Unfortunately, this was just another of the vagaries of walking mountains at night. Despite its apparently being within touching distance, it remained a long way off, and the final stretch dragged as we failed to make any impression on the distance. It seemed to be moving away from us at exactly same speed we were approaching.

When we did get there, it came as a sudden shock. We virtually stumbled on to the tumbled cairn. It had been an exhausting climb. We took a minute to drink it all in; a landscape of jagged silhouettes in every direction despite the lack of light, Loch Etive a dull, crooked silver finger bending away into the gloom. The moon was making occasional forays before dodging away again, yet the clarity in the sea of darkness was astounding.

It was at this point I noticed my compass was missing. I hadn't needed it since coming ashore and taking a reading. I thought I must have dropped it while putting on my waterproofs halfway up the ridge. As we wouldn't be going back that way, I regarded it as a write-off. Patrick had gone one better; he couldn't find his head torch. We had spares, our preparation paying off, but our apparent carelessness was surprising and annoying. With walking in the dark so often, I have become used to religiously checking the ground all round at every stopping point before moving on.

We left the summit at midnight, dropping cautiously into the jumble of the boulder field, our headlights picking up the faint path through the chaos. The dramatic drops on the right which seemed to come into view only at the last minute were a useful handrail in this dark, starless, and now moonless, night. We could make out lights from the campsite at the head of the loch thousands of feet below, and someone there must have been able to make our lights heading along the ridge, because we were suddenly hit by green laser lights from below. They kept it up for a few minutes before they became bored or maybe we had disappeared from their line of sight as we dropped.

When we reached a gentler section of the ridge, we stopped for a bite to eat. This may have technically been supper or even breakfast, but then who eats sandwiches and crisps for breakfast? This was more a meal in the realms of those returning home from a bender. I'd forgotten how long this ridge took to descend, and every new section brought a tired realisation we still had a way to go. At one point we lost the path momentarily, at another we passed a large tent pitched for the night, invisible in the dark until the last minute. The last section of descent was through deep, rocky trenches, water constantly running. The noise of the rushing Allt Mheuran below increased with every step but that only racked up the frustration. Weariness was setting in big time; we needed to reach ground level to recoup, to give the legs some respite before we tackled the final seven kilometres back to the canoe.

It was a relief when we hit the path. We took a short break to stretch the arms and legs, and grab a quick bite to sustain us for the last leg and then we were off on the path through the grasslands down to the shore. The cloud had started to organise and there was moisture in the air. The rain wasn't far away, the hoped-for pre-sunrise light nowhere in sight. The path turned south by the River Etive, the terrain waterlogged and heavy. At times it disappeared among deep vegetation, no choice but to step on to ground you knew wasn't there, another soggy step with water coming over the top of the boots. There was a fine drizzle when we reached more consistent ground and then the bothy at Kinlochetive loomed out of the gloom. This building used to operate as an open shelter, but now it is off-limits to the general public. It is leased to Venture Scotland for outdoor projects with youngsters. There was a bench at the front door with an overhang and we sat out of the rain for a few minutes. Nearby was a recently constructed shelter with a natural earth oven and benches. Despite its open-plan appearance, it looked like it would provide a warmer welcome than the run-down bothy.

The last four kilometres were a silent trudge, every ounce of energy committed to putting one foot in front of the other. The walk had that never-ending feel, the last stretch along the sliding cobbles of the shoreline, so it came as a pleasant surprise when we virtually tripped over the canoe. There was another unexpected consolation when we were preparing for the paddle home. I walked a few metres up the track to find a restroom and found my compass lying amidst the ferns. Patrick also came up trumps while he was changing clothes and his missing head torch fell out of the hood of his jacket.

The centre of the loch was choppy, but either side looked calmer. The wind was coming straight down the glen, a cold and wet front channelled through the cleavage of the mountains and picking a line down the water. The logic was to take a different route back over the loch. This time we would push straight through the rougher stuff and out into calmer waters, then travel north in the shelter of the western shore. The turbulence was more notable than on the way in, but apart from a few splashes over the side and the light drizzle, we stayed mainly dry. As we neared the finish line, I began to feel the burn in my shoulders. My arms felt heavy and I was glad that the paddling was gentler. I wondered how Patrick was feeling. As if he had read my mind, he asked: "How are you feeling?"

"A bit shattered. I need this to finish."

"Good to hear it. I feel the same."

It appeared that while the canoeing had worn me out, the night climb had done the same for Patrick. We had been on the go for more some 14 hours, including ten hours on the hill. It was a tough shift. As I drove away from the campsite, Patrick settled down in the front seat of his van for a sleep. He told me he had loved the experience but that it wasn't likely to become a new way of life. It had taken more than he had expected. I had heard this sentiment expressed before on many occasions and I would hear it again.

10
After the Cold Rush

HARVEST MOON

(Tuesday, September 25, 03.52)
Mountain: *Beinn a' Ghlo*
Soundtrack: *Harvest Moon – Neil Young*
Celebratory drink: *Harvest Ale*

Heading up the A9 late at night, just me and that man of many moons, Neil Young. My choices were limited in many respects, but the soundtrack for the Harvest Moon couldn't have been anything else.

Young eschews organised religion and instead has followed a lunar pathway during his career, taking inspiration from the moon to guide him. It shows up frequently in his work. He has recorded more than two dozen songs with lyrics making reference to the moon. He has also written many songs during its cycle, including one album where he knocked out ten tracks on one full moon night. As a musician, Neil Young is the undisputed man in the moon, the perfect travelling companion for the Harvest Moon.

This is the full moon which is closest to the autumnal equinox, so every three years it rises in October rather than September. The Harvest Moon isn't like the other moons. Throughout the year, moonrise is around 50 minutes later each day, but the difference is only about 30 minutes near the equinox. The full Harvest Moon rises at sunset and will rise around the same time for several nights. This is because the difference is at its yearly minimum, and as a result it can appear there are full moons for many nights in a row. It means an abundance of bright moonlight early in the evening, a boon to farmers harvesting summer-grown crops. Some cultures refer to it as the Barley or Corn Moon, while the Chinese call it the Chrysanthemum Moon (their Harvest Moon is in August). The ancient Celts knew it as the Singing Moon. It seems Neil Young was in harmony with them as well.

I was heading for Beinn a' Ghlo, that elegant mountain of three Munros which sits above Blair Atholl. It wasn't my first choice, but this was an outing that had to be shoehorned in between storms.

The previous week had seen destructive winds that restricted mountain walks in much of the country. First we took a pounding from Storm Ali. I had a particularly close encounter with it. I had been delivering a talk to a club in Newport-on-Tay as the tempest gathered strength and I just made it back home before the Tay Bridge was shut to vehicles. A few days later it was Storm Bronagh's turn to come raging in. We were four days on from that assault, but the winds were still lively enough to cause problems.

The naming of storms has been common in the US and Caribbean for a long time, but it's a relatively new here. The Met Office, in conjunction with its Irish counterpart Met Eireann, introduced the system after the destructive St Jude's

Day storm of 2013 which was attributed to 17 deaths in Europe, as a way to raise public awareness of the dangers. It would also avoid the confusion of referring to the remnants of hurricanes spinning across the Atlantic by their former US names.

My ideal mountain for this walk had been A' Mhaighdean, 'The Maiden', a reference not to its purity but because it is said to look from some angles like a bound stook of corn (the last sheaf to be cut at harvest was called the maiden). Poetic that may have been, and it is a grand peak, but it's a long way in and out, and with more wet and stormy conditions piling into the west I didn't fancy a hike of 12 hours or more. Besides, there are also two river crossings which can prove difficult, even uncrossable, in wet conditions.

I wasn't too put out by the idea of switching away from Fisherfield. I had enjoyed many great walks in this area and just a couple of years earlier had caught the moon here during a sunset to sunrise walk in perfect conditions centred on an ascent of A' Mhaighdean. For all but the super fit, these are hills to be enjoyed over a couple of days, wild camping along the way. I prefer to travel light and because of the oppressive heat, I wanted to carry as little as possible on this latest round. I had a lightweight tent in case of emergency, but my intention was to stay over in a rocky howff between dusk and dawn. I wanted to end the first day with a sunset and start the next with a sunrise. It would feel like an ending and a beginning.

I set off around 2pm. The heat immediately felt oppressive but there was a strong wind. The walk from this direction starts at the descent to Shenavall bothy. The first hazard, the notorious Abhainn Strath na Sealga, was inconsequential, its waters running low. The recent dry spell also meant that the usual squelch across the next kilometre or so to the next crossing at Larachantivore was a few levels down in sogginess, and a boulder was enough to cross the river running down Gleann na Muice.

I swung west into Gleann na Muice Beag, a superbly engineered path skirting round Beinn Dearg Mor and into the lonely confines above Loch Beinn Dearg. There were deer feeding here and the run of a small waterfall was being converted into a whirling ball of fine mist by the wind.

The route levelled out alongside a series of lochs with Ruadh Stac Mor and then A' Mhaighdean thrusting into the spotlight. For a while you seem to be going away from these mountains but then the path splits and turns up by Fuar Loch Mor, disintegrating more and more underfoot the higher you rise. A small cairn marks the start of the difficult to spot passage through the crags and I was at the summit of Ruadh Stac Mor in 20 minutes. I descended quickly and located the howff – a safety check that it was where I remembered; I didn't want to be searching for a needle in a rocky haystack in the dark – then made my way up to A' Mhaighdean for the light show, with Ruadh Stac Mor burning red behind.

I made it to my seat for the final performance of the evening, wedged between the rocks under the tiny cairn, sheltered from the fierce wind whipping across the summits. Ahead lay what many regard as the finest mountain view in the country; the deep trench that separates the plunging line of cliffs of this remote Munro from those of the stately Corbett Beinn Lair, the Dubh Loch spilling out of the gap round to the causeway and then the larger Fionn Loch taking up the baton all the way out to a chaotic expanse of shining lochans picked out by the late sunshine.

Solar power had turned the western vista into a land of silhouette and silver, but a turn of the head in any other direction brought into focus a different picture. A pastel rainbow ribbon circled the horizon highlighting some slopes bathed in a glowing copper red, others blue, individual rocks standing out with a glint from sheets of pale scree. Then, firing out a reminder as to who the real star of this show was, a blinding show of energy from the dipping sun, the Dubh Loch now a pulsing gold nugget amid the darkness of its surroundings. It lasted seconds, a last hurrah, before the start of a graceful descent.

The red, yellow and purple horizontal line mostly held at first, the only breach bang in the centre where the ball of light looked as though it had started melting its way through the surface. The fierce yellows that had conquered every expanse of water receded, inhaled powerfully and speedily back to source. A strange lull followed, before someone lit a fire below the horizon and the world became backlit again.

The crescent moon started its shift in earnest, hanging in the evening blue, high above the late colours left by its dayshift partner. It was time to head down. The light was fading fast; slopes and bumps were losing their contours, all definitions merging into one, fields of late-lying snow glowing in the moonlight.

I didn't have far to go to reach my refuge for the night, the rough stone shelter in the col between the hills. A giant, sloping rock has become wedged at an angle, creating a dry cave with a small entrance which has been given extra man-made protection from the elements. It's small, a shelter for two men and a dog which was lucky, because when I got there I found another wanderer already tucked up for the night along with his collie. I managed to squeeze in beside them on the earth floor, a welcome reprieve from the wind.

The night was spent largely sleepless – that tends to happen when you have a rock for a pillow – but vicious gusts cracking against the walls confirmed I was wise to go underground rather than try to pitch a tent and then wake up somewhere far away, Wizard of Oz-style. It never truly got dark. I had a constant view of the stars through my rock skylight on a background somewhere between black and blue and the sickle-shaped moon shining above the snow-veined summit ridge of A' Mhaighdean.

I rose at 4am, my eyes already accustomed to the low light. I had a long way to go. The sun which had disappeared six hours ago was already wakening from its slumbers. The sky to the east was catching fire, picking out every one of distant An Teallach's spires in the burgeoning, multi-coloured glow, a prelude to the new day. The trek to the next summit, Beinn Tarsuinn, was a slow plod but I caught the ridge early and enjoyed the traverse over a series of towers more suited to a Torridon mountain, then a stroll over that curious flat, sloping rooftop that is often referred to as Table Mountain.

Slioch and Beinn Lair were busy strutting their stuff in full light, while it was A' Mhaighdean's turn to glow red. Way off to the east and south, the glens were filled with white cloud turning the blue shapes of the hills to distant islands among roiling seas.

Long shadows occupied Gleann na Muice, the hills appearing as pieces from a jigsaw, ragged blackness cutting through their familiar lines, as I toiled up the boulder slopes of Mullach Coire Mhic Fhearchair in the curious conditions, baking heat one minute, an icy wind trying to knock me off my feet the next.

By the time I was ascending the fifth Munro, Sgurr Ban, I was dressed more for a winter's day again. It wasn't just me. A lone figure coming off the summit had thought likewise, and two more sitting at the cairn also commented on the bizarre continuing temperature changes.

It only took ten minutes of descent into the white boulder

chaos to make up my mind that I wouldn't be visiting the final peak, Beinn a' Chleidheimh. There was a long way still to go and the famed Fisherfield weariness had set in. It's a long haul from here to the river, first that shattered white rock, then a series of long boiler plate slabs and finally tough heather and grass hiding all sorts of traps. I could see the long, snaking track rising ever upwards on the other side of the river, a psychologically draining sight.

A last glance down Strath na Sealga, snaking waters cutting gently through stands of yellow gorse and stripped trees, Beinn Dearg Mor hogging the attention. Over my shoulder, Sgurr Ban now looked a long way away, a distant memory already. I had captured these peaks through every minute and every mood of the day, a true mountain cycle. The thought of sullying those memories with a trudge round in constant rain, high winds and limited visibility didn't appeal. Nothing to see here, move along please. Beinn a' Ghlo was a better bet, a shorter journey and the promise of settled weather.

§

THE uncertainty of this walk's venue and timings meant I would be going solo again. It was too much work to liaise with someone else. Walking alone at night has never bothered me. I am happy to walk in company but not if it means compromising my plans. I have felt alone out on the mountains, but never lonely. The astrological signs suggested this full moon was ideal for the lone entrepreneur, great for overcoming fears and shedding inhibitions. I suppose that could also be read as the kind of advice on which the Naked Rambler based his ideology.

I'm often pulled up by friends about my lack of party planning when completing a round of hills. This is not entirely deliberate. I have been a free spirit too long; the last thing I want to do is start being responsible for organising disparate groups, not to mention refreshments for a small army. I am good at planning for one, after that it gets messy.

I had friends spending a few days walking the Cateran Trail around the time of the Harvest Moon, but there wasn't a mountain option that would have tied in. I would catch up with them a few days later. A week before the full moon, I had attended a friend's celebration of her Full House – the completion of the six main hill lists, Munros, Tops, Corbetts, Furths (the Munro-height peaks in England, Wales and Ireland), Grahams and Donalds. It's a great achievement, and the turn-out was like a Who's Who of Scottish hillwalking. Looking at the assembled group of Mountaineering Scotland and Munro Society members, mountain rescuers and various club worthies, it made the mind boggle at the thought of how many mountain rounds had been racked up in total.

Anne had chosen Fiarach, a modest hill near Tyndrum, as her final ascent. There were 56 people (and ten dogs) in the party. I doubt that Fiarach had seen that many ascents over the other 364 days of the year combined. The weather was surprisingly benign, but as we celebrated on the summit we could see the clouds organising, a warning of coming storms. We made it down just before the deluge arrived. Ali was just a few days away. No sooner had it blasted across the country, Bronagh came barrelling in. With just two days to go before the full moon, and the tail end of the storm still battering and soaking the north-west, my decision to switch from Fisherfield seemed the sane one.

Beinn a' Ghlo is an old favourite, a mountain I have known through many moods. It's easy to see why it is known as the mountain of mist. This sprawling upland of copious peaks and corries is a notorious vapour magnet. Even on the most perfect of days it can have ribbons of gauze wrapped around its shoulders, caressing the slopes like an infatuated lover, while all around its neighbours are cloud-free. Sometimes this can be the very fibre of its beauty, the constantly shifting views, the tantalising glimpses of what lies ahead.

My last night trek five years ago was a fine example. We were shooting a promotional film for the launch of *Moonwalker*, and set off around 2am hoping to capture the sunrise. The mist was clinging to the ground, the ascent to Carn Liath a series of shots of the light of my torch bobbing slowly upwards.

Reaching the summit we found only more grey, yet within minutes the mists twisted and swirled, eventually lifting like the curtain at a cinema from a bygone era to welcome in the most spectacular and colourful sunrise I have ever seen. We sat for hours, hypnotised by the cloud waterfalls pouring over the connecting ridge, the glens below filled in like endless white lagoons.

The moon seemed to be suffering from shyness as Neil and I cruised up the empty A9, but I did catch a few sightings. The turn up the minor road to Loch Moraig seemed to be like crossing the threshold into an alternate world. Gnarled and twisted trees crowded in on both sides, rabbits criss-crossing here, there and everywhere, the shrapnel of branches, earth and boulders littering the route.

By the time I arrived at Loch Moraig, the moon was nowhere to be seen but its influence was evident. The mountains ahead were standing out clearly under a mottled grey sky, the track leading to them a glowing streak. Behind the hills were white candy floss towers, distant reminders that these benign conditions were transient. There was a camper van and a couple of cars sitting in the darkness and two tents close by, but no sign of movement.

I stepped out of the car and was immediately assailed by the roaring of stags, their territorial warnings cutting through the still night. They could have been five miles away, they could have been a few hundred metres; there was no way of telling in this outdoor echo chamber. The only light, a faint twinkling coming from the farm a few miles away.

It was just before midnight, and the moon was scheduled for 3.52am. An hour or so of rest and I was gearing up for the first full moon walk of autumn. The pack was starting to feel heavy after the lazier, more settled walks of the last few months. Going out alone also made a difference; now I would have to be prepared for anything and pack accordingly. We weren't quite at the ironmongery stage of the year, but there was enough of a bite in the air to require the carrying of extra layers. Late September, on a high mountain in the middle of the night: it could be raw up there.

I was walking on a track but I needed the head torch under the moonless skies, especially across the level, boggy section which leads to the start of the mountain path up Carn Liath, the first of the peaks. This is a path that has been in need of some TLC for a long while. It has worn away badly over the years, and in some sections it is like walking in a trench filled with scree and rubble. Its scar can be seen for miles by anyone heading up the A9. The good news is that it has been neatly repaired in the lower reaches, and the Mend Our Mountains appeal should ensure the unsightly ravages higher up will soon be massaged into something more fitting for such a jewel of a mountain.

About halfway up, the Harvest Moon suddenly revealed itself and I was able to walk with the torch off. The ground below was still under the control of a drifting sheet of gauze. I sat down to take some pictures and thought I noticed a light moving steadily up the hill, about ten minutes behind me. It was too bright, too singular, to have been the eyes of an animal. A few days earlier, I had an enquiry from someone interested in joining me on the walk, but because of the uncertainty of the weather and subsequent starting times for the walk, we agreed it would be too difficult to organise. Now I began to wonder if they had been in the parked camper van, had spotted my light heading off and then decided to try to catch up. I started off again and the light kept coming. There was no sound. The wind was beginning to affect my gait, an occasional lash from its cold whip a reminder that the balmy days had been left behind. I had to halt at times and plant my poles to avoid being pushed over. Below, the light was fainter, a result of misty reinforcements blowing in.

By the time I hit the final rise, the temperature had plummeted, and the light could no longer be seen. If there had been someone there, I suspected they may have turned back, disheartened by the ever thicker cloud and stronger wind and the tricky job of walking on continually moving scree. It could all have been a trick of the light. I had seen this before during a walk on Meall Chuaich in deep snow, when it appeared someone was signalling from an outcrop in the vastness of the white above. Whatever the explanation, I never saw another sign of anyone.

I sat down inside the protective circle at one of the cairns to get out of the wind and regrouped. I was wearing six top layers and two on the bottom, a balaclava, hat and hood, winter gloves with silk liners, winter socks and boots. It may have been September, but I needed them all.

The walk towards the second summit, Braigh Coire Chruinn-bhalgain, gave me hope, the gloom lifting for a while, the moon poking through again. It was short-lived. As I continued to rise, the cloud came in thicker than before and the final push to the summit was blind. A compass reading was the only clue to my destination. The head torch had been rendered impotent, light bouncing helplessly back from the grey and black. When I reached the cairn, I abandoned any thought of heading on to the third peak. There's a kink in the ridge here, and finding the correct turn could be tricky. It's not particularly dangerous ground, more of a nuisance, but I still didn't fancy wandering around in the depths of one corrie or other in the gloom trying to figure out exactly where I was. Safer to head back the way I came and hopefully reach Carn Liath for the sunrise.

I have to admit to a degree of smugness along with relief when I arrived back at the col – another navigation test passed with flying colours. There are those who would say I could simply have used electronic mapping and completed the circuit. I've had a GPS for more than ten years, but only used it on one or two occasions. I've always regarded it as a tool for emergencies. Maybe it was the way navigation techniques were constantly drummed into me when I started, but tradition still reigns over technology for me. I usually go astray about once a year, but I've found you learn more from mistakes than simply being right all the time.

There has been a worrying increase in people having to be rescued in the mountains because they relied on smartphones for navigation. I even heard someone boasting they had been walking in Scotland for three years but hadn't once used a map or compass. After all, he said, mountain rescue teams now use up-to-date tech. That's true, but they also believe it's common sense that everyone who goes out on the hills should be able to use a map and compass.

Then there are those who go out without any form of navigation tools at all, relying simply on following a hill path. I'm dismayed at how many times the dazed and confused assume a stranger is willing and able to lead them to safety. I have no problem helping out but sometimes the belligerence is astounding, as if it is your duty.

I was leading a party in the Grey Corries when a guy came out of the mist. He had a big white beard and looked the part but there was no doubt he was lost.

He looked at the group then asked: "Are you a guide?"

I told him 'No' and he looked put out. Then he bellowed: "You look like a guide."

I could have told him he looked like Captain Bird's Eye, but I wouldn't go around assuming he was carrying fish fingers in his backpack.

I've often wondered that with the pace of technology if, say, 20 or so years from now, there will be anyone left doing the hills using paper maps. It may be the inevitable result of progress but it would be a shame. I've always regarded maps as things of beauty that should be treasured. I often spend hours poring over them, plotting routes, finding intrigue in the discovery of unusual and remote spots.

I was a cartophile from a young age. We sketched out a map, then soaked it overnight in salt water to give it a sepia tinge. When it was dried out it looked aged, an ancient guide to pirate treasure. Sometimes we would even use a cigarette lighter to singe the edges for an extra touch of authenticity. There's still that childlike feeling when I look at the detail on a new map. There's more to it than nostalgia: I simply love the challenge on the hills. While I appreciate the extra safety and comfort that some devices can provide, there's nothing to beat working it all out the old-fashioned way by recognising the run of the contours and the lie of the land.

So am I anti-tech? Not guilty, M'Luddite.

I find it interesting how some people are prepared to shrug off the past and embrace new tech wholeheartedly while others of the same generation shun it. Then there are those who cherry pick. For instance, I love books, but I also have a Kindle. I resisted for many years. I still prefer a book and will always buy a print copy ahead of any electronic version. My semi-conversion came when a friend was in hospital and I realised how much easier it was to have a constant stream of reading material that didn't involve moving large suitcases. It's handy for holidays and travelling, and sometimes to pick up books no longer in print. That's as far as it goes. I will not surrender to a literary life in the ether.

Some friends still refuse to have them. One even said he felt it was a betrayal to authors then immediately switched on his iPod to listen to music without a shred of irony. At least I still have my vinyl collection. Despite the new challengers, books and vinyl records have seen a resurgence, and it's not just about nostalgia. They are still the best and purest mediums for their art. I suspect that at some point in the future the same will happen with maps.

The deep dip at the col proved to be an eye in the centre of the fury. It provided some respite, but also a slightly false sense of security. I knew I would feel the true features of this night as soon I started climbing again. A horizontal strip of blazing red in the east promised better times, but I was certain it was a false dawn. The truth lay a few hundred feet ahead; I was quickly back into the cloud and rampaging wind.

The consolation in walking alone in zero visibility can be found in the small details. There was no point in looking ahead, none in searching for views. Instead, with the reduced vision, I looked down at my feet. I was walking on a vividly-coloured carpet of surprises, short-clipped russet grass with sprouting patches of green and purple, the odd rock sparkling silver under the beam of the torch. There was a bounce, a sponginess that belied the high mountain setting; I felt I could have taken off my boots and walked barefoot quite happily. I made it back to the first summit in time but the sunrise was hidden by the all-enveloping mists. There was the occasional promise of a light show to come, and for a few seconds the mist took on a pulsating orange glow, hypnotic and slightly spooky, but it never developed any further. I sat it out at the cairn for around 45 minutes, tucked in against the worst excesses of the wind. I tried to pass the time by trying to count as many different shades I could in the rocks of the cairn walls.

Every so often I would peep round the corner to see if progress was being made, but in the end my optimism counted for nothing and all I got was a feeling akin to frostbite. It was time to call it a day. The night had been disappointing in many ways, but I had achieved what I had set out to do. When the roofs and walls were shaking over the past week, the idea of reaching a Munro summit had seemed an impossible dream. I had been on the mountain for six hours and was still in one piece. Despite a night that provided merely a fleeting interaction with the full moon, Beinn a' Ghlo had still proved to be a realm for the senses.

About half an hour after I dropped down from the summit the cloud started to shift. I consoled myself with the thought that had I stayed up there this would never have happened. Slowly the morning came to life; the wind started to ease, the mountain tops cleared, the landscape a patchwork quilt of autumnal shades, green, yellow, brown as far as the eye could see.

There were several pairs of walkers on the way up, nodding a hello to the strange, dishevelled man sitting at the side of the path, eating breakfast No.2 and looking as though he had just spent the night on the mountain.

11
The Nadir Hunter

HUNTER'S MOON

(Wednesday, October 24, 17.45)
Mountain*: Lochnagar: Cac Carn Beag*
Soundtrack*: The Hunter – Free*
Celebratory drink*: Sharpshooter wheat beer*

We walked into the heart of Lochnagar, roaring all around. The guns may have fallen silent for the stag shooting season, but these monarchs of the glen were still vociferous in the last days of their rut. It seemed they were giving us their seal of approval for our moon walk. The roaring wasn't all down to the stags. The wind was also laying claim to the night, bellowing and battering, moaning and groaning, like it had seemed to have been doing for more than six weeks. The screaming would come later.

The Hunter's Moon is the first full moon after the Harvest Moon, so, like its predecessor, it can also fall later some years in November. The name is self-explanatory; the brightness of this moon was said to make it easy for hunters to spot their prey during the race to stock the larder before the onset of the lean winter months. It is also sometimes referred to as the Blood Moon. No prizes for guessing why.

We were hoping to catch a clear night in our crosshairs on the mountain jewel of Royal Deeside and for a couple of hours it looked promising. In the end we were treated to an acted-out version of Lord Byron's seminal poem Dark Lochnagar, with its gales, stormy mists, tempests and steep, frowning glories. You could call it a form of poetic justice.

I was joined by long-time mountain pals Robert and Susan. I was glad of their company. The last walk on Beinn a' Ghlo had felt like a tipping point in the programme. The nights were drawing in fast, a definite feel we heading back into the early darkness. The long, lazy walks from April through to August were behind me. There were only three walks to complete the year but it was starting to feel like a chore. After rising from the depths of winter and hitting the summer highs, I felt I was spiralling down again, approaching the nadir.

When I was walking regularly at night, it was based around my work hours and lifestyle. It was tiring, but it was a good tiredness, a mental refreshment, and it meant I could get out more. Now, with my walking hours completely at odds with a 'normal' life, it took more of an effort to force myself out. The result was that I was beginning to resent it and weariness was quicker to set in. Going solo did not hold any great appeal now – I was happy to have fellow travellers.

I was also interested to get their take on the night walking experience. Robert was the first person to brave my night walks but the last one had been about 20 years ago. He had been a good climber and had bags of mountain experience, but he also had bad memories of being on the hills at night.

His first night-time foray had been more by accident

than design, and it could have ended in disaster. He and a friend had set off at noon on a freezing November day to try to reach Ossian's Cave, that black slit high on the rock face of Aonach Dubh in Glen Coe. His pal was determined to sign the visitor book in the cave, despite Robert's repeated warnings that they had left it too late in the day. He insisted on carrying on regardless, and Robert felt it would be folly to separate so on they went.

They had a rope, carabiners, canvas belay straps and a torch. After signing the book, they started to descend in the rapidly fading light. This entailed four abseil pitches with only the torch to see where they were going. They noticed cars down in the glen stopping because they could see the light above, wondering if someone was in trouble in such a precarious position at this late hour.

When they finally made it down and arrived at the Clachaig, the barman shouted: "Are you the guys who were up at Ossian's Cave in the dark?"

When they owned up, he told them in front of a crowded bar, that had they been five minutes later, the Glencoe rescue team would have been on their way up to get them.

It's hardly surprising that Robert seemed hesitant when I invited him out for a night foray in Glen Shiel. His biggest problem this time was the travelling in the early hours. I had to stop the car on a couple of occasions for him to throw up. Once we arrived in Glen Shiel at 4am, with the early sun brushing across the ridges in golden waves, his demeanour changed. He had never experienced a dawn on a mountain and he found it exhilarating. It was to be the catalyst to more night adventures. Whereas Robert was still tidying the last of his Munros, Susan had done them all, but this was her debut night. I was intrigued by the prospect of two people coming at this with wildly differing experiences.

I left home under blue skies filled with honking skeins of geese for a meet in Blairgowrie at lunchtime, and a stop at the Cateran Cafe to take on board as many calories as possible. We had allowed more than enough time for a leisurely drive through Glenshee and Braemar to Ballater, but got caught in a series of road diversions just to get out of the town. Further on, we had to make another detour, this time at Bridge of Cally where a section of the road to Glenshee was shut. This time, the alternative route was an upgrade on the intended one, a greener, fresher run towards the picturesque village of Kirkmichael and then a loop back north-east to pick up the Glenshee road.

It seemed to be rush hour on the B-road from Ballater to the car park at Loch Muick, but all the other vehicles were heading out. There were still a few stragglers, most preparing to pack up. We felt the wind as soon as we stepped out of the car, the psithurism almost symphonic, but the forecast was for an easing of the gales that had been with us since the passing of Storm Callum 12 days earlier. It was also suggested the strongest blasts would not be over the summits. I suspected that if the forecasts of 65mph gusts were accurate, we would struggle to reach the top of the mountain. I approached two walkers who looked like they had just been on the heights and asked them how their day had gone.

"We never got near the summit. We were being blown off our feet, took a real battering."

Not what I wanted to hear, but I thanked them and returned to get my gear on in the dying light of the day. They gave us some curious looks: I suppose the summation of their day made them think we would just drive away.

We weren't on a suicide mission. The wind would be a problem, but if it proved too much of one, we were prepared to turn back. At least a dry night was forecast. The combination of high winds and heavy rain or driving snow can be lethal.

It wasn't as if this would be a new experience. I had taken a beating on Beinn a' Ghlo, and had been out in similar conditions a few times since. The conveyor belt of storms from the Atlantic can be running at full pelt in September and October, but you can also find some of the calmest days' walking during this time in the eye of the storms.

Shortly after the Harvest Moon walk, I had decanted to Carbost in Skye for a few days with my mountain club. The forecast did not look kind. I stopped off en route to squeeze in a walk before the furies were unleashed. There was a damp, eerie calm as I made my way up Glen Arnisdale, the Highland cows ganged together in anticipation, their unruly ginger hair blending in sympathetically with the autumnal backdrop of the steep slopes on either side of the glen. Two bridge crossings, complete with curious warning signs: No Horses. My pack was heavy, something for every eventuality, but a horse was one of the few things I hadn't packed. That really could have ruined the day. By the time I was on the way out, the rain was sweeping in. By the time I reached my Skye base, the typhoon was in full voice.

The following day was the type where everyone sits tight. The guides cancelled en masse, thoughts of the Cuillin ridge an aberration. As is so often the case in Scotland, the gales and heavy rain pounding us were localised. I took my chances and travelled 50 miles east to Killilan, wrapped in as much waterproofing as I could manage, and then splashed my way through the woods and out of the cloud and rain. It was breezy, but it was at my back and it drove me along and then up the ridge to the summit of Carn na Breabaig. It felt strange walking back into the ambush of towering black clouds and persistent rain.

We ventured on to the ridge the next day when the winds had eased slightly, up in the shelter of the boulders of the Sgumain stone chute. When we emerged on the ridge for the final push to Sgurr Sgumain, we found ourselves in a snow storm which only eased at the summit. Sgurr Alasdair, until now hidden from view, suddenly reared up like Godzilla bursting forth from the ocean, eliciting gasps at its domineering presence. As we dropped over the col into Coir' a' Ghrunnda, the sun came out, picking out every drop of moisture on every slab and rock face, creating a gargantuan hall of mirrors. The day of four seasons produced a grand finale, a sunlit double rainbow arch at the entrance to Coire Lagan, the peaks behind dark and threatening, the rain thundering down, yet we were bathed in sunshine.

§

THIS meteorological mash-up of a month meant a change of plan on the next outing, a trip over Loch Linnhe into the Munro-free zone of Ardgour. This is prime deer stalking territory, and although we were only a few days away from the end of the season, they can often be the busiest. I made contact with the head stalker at the Ardgour estate and was given the all-clear on my route in Glen Tarbert in a swift and helpful response. My planned circuit of Beinn Mheadhoin at Kingairloch, however, was likely to be more problematic due to the bottleneck approach to the hill. If there is shooting here, there is no real alternative to the route. The dilemma was taken out of my hands when I discovered that part of entry road had collapsed a few days earlier under mudslides.

The open season for stags in Scotland is statutory and runs from July 1 to October 20. Most sporting estates won't start culling until the stags are in hard antler, sometime around mid-August. The peak period is in the breeding season from mid to late September. The stags use up much of their fat and energy reserves during the rut and are in poor condition. They need to take on plenty of nutrition quickly before winter sets in, so they are left undisturbed as much as possible from October 20 to give them the best chance for winter survival.

The open season for hinds is from October 21 to February 15. This is said to allow a better chance of any calf that has lost its mother to survive, although it is often the case that the calf is culled with the hind to avoid leaving an orphan so early in the season. After mid-February the weather and shortage of feed make survival the main challenge until spring.

Deer culling is an emotive subject, but numbers have grown exponentially in the past few decades and they do need to be controlled. It's one of the arguments consistently put forward for the re-introduction of apex predators, such as bears, wolves and lynx. A hard, frozen winter can mean a high casualty rate, with food hard to reach through the depths of solid snow. A wet winter can prove just as catastrophic for the animals, the precipitation from constant heavy sleet and rain penetrating their coats instead of building up an insulating cover. Stalkers say they do their best to select older beasts and those in poor condition for culling in a bid to minimise natural mortality and also to try to ensure the best welfare for the surviving animals.

Not everyone plays by the same rules. An American hunter, Larysa Switlyk, caused outrage when she posted pictures of herself and a client posing with a goat and other animals they had shot on Islay. Legally, she had done nothing wrong. She had been granted a licence for culling on the island. It came as a surprise to many that freelance hunters were permitted to go around the country picking off the wildlife. It may even have slipped by unnoticed if it hadn't been for the offensive, self-congratulatory gloating of this trophy hunter. It's not as if she had fought in hand-to-claw combat with a tiger or wrestled a giant python; this 'big-game' hunter shot a goat and a sheep. If all she wanted was a picture she could probably have walked up to the animals and got them to pose for a selfie.

One stalker told me some of the blame for this increasing free-for-all could be put down to the slashing of forestry budgets. He said fencing repair funds had been cut, and that was allowing many more deer to be drawn into commercial woodlands where they could be shot throughout the year irrespective of season, age or condition.

He said it seemed crazy that having spent pounds erecting fences, there was then a refusal to spend pennies keeping them in good order. This allows the deer to be drawn into the woodlands where they cause damage to the trees before being shot. The costs in damage to the woodlands and of these culls far outweighed the savings from the fencing repair budget.

He also told me that sporting estates observed the closed seasons and shot in daylight only, leaving the hills quiet for the deer whose main feeding time is at night. But elsewhere there are out-of-season, indiscriminate shoot-on-sight policies – including shooting throughout the night using night vision aids. He reckoned this was adversely affecting the welfare, age and social structure of herds, and threatening the jobs of people on the estates and in tourism.

I had an interesting conversation on the hill with a guy whose son was a stalker. He said they were having an argument from differing viewpoints over stag shooting when his son asked: "Do you eat venison?"

As the answer was 'Yes' he was then asked: "So you are happy for someone else to do the killing?"

He said that made him feel like a hypocrite. If he was

going to eat venison, then at least he should be prepared to find out what it entailed. The upshot was that he found himself going along on a stalk with his son. They shot a stag, took it off the hill, dressed and prepared it. He said he was glad he had gone along, but he didn't enjoy the experience and wouldn't repeat it. He didn't stop eating venison, though.

I was still knee-deep in deer during my Ardgour outing, a long horseshoe circuit of Coire an Iubhair with an out-and-back peak tacked on. This walk was so autumnal it should have carried an October copyright. The landscape was wall to wall russet, skies pale grey, mists drifting languidly across the midriff of the mountains. Sometimes they ventured higher, hiding the summits, sometimes they sank to fill in the glens, a sea of cotton wool to make you feel like a marooned sailor. The walls of Garbh Bheinn seemed impregnable, dark towers reaching above the cloud. The only thing missing was an eagle drifting along in the thermals.

From every direction came the roaring of stags. The first volley sounded like fingernails being scraped across a corrugated metal tray. They were just getting warmed up. The cacophony built over the next couple of hours until there was a wall of sound, sometimes a roar, other times a loud bark or deep lowing. They imitated chainsaws, out-of-tune cars starting up, and, at one point, Brian Blessed. It sounded like a party to celebrate the end of the hunting season.

It brought back memories of an October night ascent in Mull, when I had climbed Ben More to finish my third round of Munros. My two previous finishes had been celebrated with friends. This time I wanted to go alone, to ascend in the darkness, the light rising with me, just as I did so often over 15 years of solo night walking.

I wanted to sit in silent contemplation drinking in the morning light, thinking about all the hill days that had led to this point, all the great memories of lost friends who never managed to make it this far.

I fell asleep under clear skies around midnight at the side of Loch na Keal. When I woke two hours later, all visibility was gone, swallowed up by a cloying mist. The head torch was useless, its light more of a nuisance as it bounced back from the grey. I could see nothing, but I could hear plenty. The haunting bellows of stags, somewhere ahead. It was unsettling: there was no telling how near or far they were. It would be no laughing matter to stumble across a large male looking for a fight. There was a primal beauty in those roars. The deer belonged here – I was the interloper. Yet I made it up and down without ever seeing one of them.

§

THERE had been a few mountain options for the Hunter's Moon. Slioch, for example, 'The Spear', that impregnable looking fortress of rock that towers above Loch Maree. There was Sgurr nan Conbhairean in Glen Shiel, with its connections to hunters and their dogs. Again, it was the prospect of better weather in the eastern half of the country that made up my mind. Lochnagar, its tradition of hunting and monarchs, both human and ruminant, was the logical choice.

The mountain's name has been taken from the loch in its north-east corrie, Lochan na Gaire, 'little loch of noisy sound'. The original name was Beinn na Ciochan, 'hill of the paps', a reference to the prominent points of the twin summits.

Now here we were, the shadows of the coming night already starting to spread across the ground, the breeze reminding us of what could lie ahead. We heard owls calling as we walked through the wood, adding to the constant bellowing that was reverberating all around. The top of the mountain was visible, an irrelevant, wispy intrusion of cloud hanging around. The horizon behind was calm and beautifully backlit, autumn shades morphing through subtle layers. The one ahead was darker, but once we reached the levelling of the track the sudden change was breathtaking.

The mountain heights were black silhouettes, the high dappled cloud under the blue canvas throbbing red and purple and yellow jagged veins were stitching it all together. A matter of minutes and it had changed to softer toned waves of ochre on a pale blue background. Behind us, the sky had taken on the look of a portending alien invasion, roiling clouds burned orange in their turbulence. It was as though we were starring in a Scottish remake of *Independence Day*. My excitement was building at what we would find when we reached the loch higher in the corrie.

Except, with the flick of a switch, it was gone. At one point, there was a glow on the distant horizon, the moon appearing like the eyeball of a great dragon slowly opening one eye, but it quickly slammed shut. All we had was darkness. We took a short break for refreshments before reaching the lip of the corrie, head torches like searchlights making sure we hadn't dropped or misplaced anything.

The speed with which the last chink of light had vanished was astonishing. I had hoped to make the short detour over to the loch in the hope of catching the moon shining down on the water but it was difficult to gauge our progress in the blackness, so much so that we were already climbing the rock staircase known as The Ladder without realising we had risen so far. We were also taking a battering.

The corrie bowl was being scoured by the wind, the inability to escape its confines increasing the power of the maelstrom. The result was an unpredictability of where the next blow would come from.

We were like mismatched boxers, taking punches from one direction and then, when we tried to compensate, to ready ourselves for the next punch, it would land from another improbable angle.

We were being knocked back and forth, at some points off our feet. We found ourselves on all fours, the easiest way to make headway. We were also going offline, but there was nothing we could about it and anyway, there was better shelter where we were being forced. I fully expected to see one of us lifted off our feet and carried off the hill in ever increasing circles until vanishing completely.

We huddled in for a moment, to get our breath back for the next push, but also to rethink our plan. We were close to the top of the climb. If the wind was as fierce up there in the open, we would retreat. We were a little punch-drunk when we topped out, but the wind speed was dramatically reduced. It felt strange to be able to walk upright again. We decided to push on. The path curved to the north as it rose to the plateau but this was easier walking despite a drizzling mist blowing across. On the way we noticed a message carved into a sandy section of the track. It read: It's a bit blowy.

As we crossed the plateau, a bevy of ptarmigan appeared ahead in the gloom, tiny, shadowy figures confused by this interruption, scuttling in every direction. It was a mass scuttling. The wind was building in strength again and we were glad of the shelter among the huge boulders that house the trig point on Cac Carn Beag, the main summit. We did the usual gear recce before we stepped back out into the elements. This was when Robert noticed that his map, case and compass were missing from the back of his rucksack. Despite being tightly secured, they must have been ripped away by the sheer force of the gale during our ascent of The Ladder without any of us noticing.

As we made our way off the plateau, the moon made a fleeting appearance above the cairn on Cac Carn Mor and we raced to capture the moment. A few quick snaps of a hooded figure standing in illuminated, exaggerated drops of rain, and that was our lot. The visibility was now zero, the wind and incessant moisture reducing the scope of our torches. We went off line a little, partly because we wanted to be sure we wouldn't turn right too soon and end up near the edge of the ring of cliffs. We had been following Robert's phone app map, but had also backed this up with my paper map and compass readings. The importance of this was underlined when the phone died suddenly with the battery wiped out by the cold.

We found our way back to the path by compass. A few hundred feet down and we were out of the worst. A few hundred feet more and we were starting to enjoy the breeze as respite from the extra clothing layers we had needed higher up. There was an undeniable feeling of relief now that we had left the furore behind on the mountain. We had felt the potential of the tempest but it could have been much worse.

The random gusts continued, some of the strongest of the night coming as we dropped past the series of waterfalls and neared the lochside. There seemed no rhyme nor reason to these winds. The clarity of the night was impressive, the shapes and contours standing out in all directions, but hopes of a late appearance from the moon shining on the waters of the loch came to nothing. Dark Lochnagar had lived up to its billing.

Susan had approached this walk with a mixture of excitement and mild trepidation, but in the end it had been a night of surprises for her. She had been surprised how much light there was despite the moon being parked behind cloud for most of the walk. She was surprised at how much wildlife she had seen, and how she could walk at midnight on a track without needing a torch.

She reckoned she had walked in far worse visibility during daylight and that it felt less different to a day walk than she had expected. She was also surprised how much of a sensory experience it had been. Her other senses had more than compensated for the lack of sight.

She loved being able to pick out the lights of distant settlements which would otherwise remained unseen in daylight, and she loved seeing the shimmering waters of Loch Muick from hundreds of feet above.

As she so succinctly put it: "That was less mad than I had imagined."

Robert's take was entirely different. He had felt more relaxed about the walk because of his previous undertakings. He had done it once, he could do it again. He had also built up a wealth of experience in the navigational and technical aspects of mountain walking over the intervening years, and was walking with two other highly competent walkers. He had no worries about the prospects of getting lost or his being unable to last the distance.

So it was surprising to hear he felt the Lochnagar walk was "without question the toughest challenge I have ever undertaken". One reason was that we were starting and finishing in the dark, whereas the walks we did in the mid 1990s were more sedate. We would normally begin in the dark and travel through sunrise into the full light of day. He said the constant darkness brought back unwanted memories of his Ossian's Cave nightmare.

The weather was also a factor. Because we could pick and choose, previous night walks had generally been in calm, high-pressure conditions with superb visibility which lifted a lot of the worry of something going wrong. Now here we were in limited visibility, the ferocity of the gales knocking you sideways every second step. The contrast couldn't have been greater.

One other thing to take into account may have been the reports of two recent Cairngorms incidents. In the preceding two weeks, mountain rescue teams had been called out to help several people who had become lost or got into difficulties during storms with wind speeds topping 70mph. Some did not have proper clothing and others were relying on maps on their phones without the back-up of map and compass. Robert said it was at the back of his mind that if we had got into difficulties and needed to be rescued, people would be critical of anyone being on a mountain in such conditions at that time of night.

His final verdict, once safely back at the car, was one of invigoration, a satisfaction that it was a successful conclusion on a mountain expedition that few might experience.

The pace of the final yomp along the lochside belied what had gone before, the adrenaline rush kicking in with the realisation we were almost there. We had a momentary spot of panic when we noticed blue lights in the car park, fearing someone had seen the lone car and phoned the rescue services, but it turned out just to be the lights on the parking meters. The road out was deserted and we didn't see another vehicle until Glenshee. I was home and in bed before 4am.

A week later I was on Lochnagar again, this time during daylight and approaching from a different direction, but the wind hadn't appeared to have moved on; it was still ripping across the slopes with no mercy. It felt rather strange to be able to pick where we had been during the hours of darkness, where we had climbed and where we had gone offline. It provided some perspective to the whole walk. It was like seeing the mountain with fresh eyes.

12
The Darkest Night

BEAVER MOON

(Friday, November 23, 05.39)
Mountain: *Ben Cruachan*
Soundtrack: *Mountains of the Moon – Grateful Dead*
Celebratory drink: *Beavertown Gamma Ray pale ale*

There's a story that rolls round every couple of years suggesting the Earth will be plunged into 15 days of absolute darkness in November. One theory is that this will be caused by a collision between Jupiter and Venus, triggering a chain reaction that will block the light of the sun. Another is that a comet will pass between Earth and the sun.

These disaster scenarios are much loved by conspiracy theorists, and are often backed by 'confirmation' from NASA. Fake news, but I did begin to question whether there might just be a smidgen of truth in this during our night ascent for the November full moon.

The eleventh month always feels the darkest of the year. It may not have the least hours of daylight, but try telling that to the human psyche which is blindsided by the dramatic change in balance between light and dark. It's the element of surprise; our bodies and minds haven't yet become fully attuned to the sudden switch to winter hours. The clocks go back, night comes faster.

The change is striking. You have what seems like a two-minute warning before the black curtain crashes down, smothering the last flickers of illumination. It's a different kind of darkness from the summer and early autumn months, more absolute, more enveloping. It instantly snuffs out any remaining heat of the day; the drop in temperature is formidable.

I'm no stranger to night forays into the mountains, but I find walks from mid-November until the end of December the most psychologically challenging. The walk out in freezing darkness is when the comfort zone shifts, the only time I feel alone in the outdoors.

Perhaps it's the initial shock to the system caused by the speed that light is extinguished, or simply the realisation that we are now on the unstoppable descent towards the shortest day. It's not the time to discover you have forgotten to check your head torch before venturing out.

Suddenly, distances seem expanded, sanctuary and warmth a long way off. When you do finally arrive back at the car, there is much shivering, more haste but less speed.

You hurry to remove the cold, wet gear and get into warm clothes and the heat of the interior, but it always seems to put up more of a fight at this time of year.

Gaiters get stuck, boot laces refuse to become unknotted. Socks feel painted on to your feet, every under-layer superglued to your body. Removal turning into forced eviction.

It eventually comes away in limp, sodden pieces, dropping

from trembling hands, some on the ground, some flung carelessly into the car. Some will remain lost, left behind in the dark or blowing away in the slipstream when you drive off. Some will be recovered later when they send out an SOS from underneath the seats with that overpowering smell of rotten turnips. I'm sure that some poor sods who have accepted a lift may have been left with the impression that I transport farm animals around the country in my spare time.

I was under no illusion that the walk for the penultimate full moon would be the darkest so far. This was the time of year when the beavers built their winter dams. It was also the last chance for hunters to trap the animals for meat and pelts before the lakes were frozen over until spring. It is sometimes known as the Frost Moon and the Chinese call it the White Moon, but the Celtic name is the most appropriate: The Dark Moon.

I still had hopes that I could squeeze my favourite mountain, An Teallach, into the programme and the fact that November 23 is also St Clement's Day provided a possible link. Pope Clement I is the patron saint of blacksmiths and metalworkers, so climbing 'The Forge' on the night of the full moon would satisfy my self-imposed criteria.

The name is said to derive from travellers seeing the sun glinting on mists creeping up the massive faces of the mountain, conjuring thoughts of sparks flying from the anvils of blacksmiths working below. From a distance, An Teallach can appear like a volcano, a dark pall rising into otherwise clear skies, a vision of smoke and fury. I have enjoyed many great days on – and under – this mountain, and the thought of catching that wonderful serrated skyline under a brilliant moon was exciting. Then it got complicated.

The Scots Magazine had been covering my full moon progress on their website from the beginning, and Rob and

Katrina, both experienced walkers, were keen to see for themselves. Either that, or they were just making sure that I really was climbing these mountains as I had said and not just photographing a pile of rocks in my garden under cover of darkness and poor visibility.

I had also invited Rachael, a New Zealander working as a mountain guide in Scotland. Now the logistics were more intricate. Rob and Katrina would be coming from Dundee, Rachael from Glasgow. There was also the further complication of my own schedule. I had a double-header of book talks over the two days and was due at the Dundee Mountain Film Festival later that evening. An Teallach is a long way off for an overnight walk, especially when you can't guarantee the weather. I would have to think again.

Then, a flash of inspiration. There might not be mountains with any direct reference to beavers, but beavers build dams and there is a choice when it comes to dams. Ben Cruachan would be ideal, about half the travelling time of An Teallach and easier access for all involved.

I had planned to at least make a nod to the beaver by travelling down to the nearby Knapdale Forest and following the beaver trail before catching up with the others at Cruachan.

The Scottish Beaver Trial, a five-year study to prove how the animals could enhance and restore natural environments, was given the go-ahead in 2008. It was introduced in Argyll the following year in a partnership between the Scottish Wildlife Trust, The Royal Zoological Society of Scotland and Forestry Commission Scotland.

Beavers were native to Scotland until around 400 years ago, but they were hunted to extinction for their fur and a glandular oil secreted from the base of their tail. In medieval times the oil, castoreum, was used as a treatment for headaches. The beaver is regarded as a keystone species in the natural world. They build dams in rivers and lodges in ponds. Their dammed water attracts species such as frogs, toads, water voles, otters, dragonflies, birds and fish. The trial was deemed a success and in 2016 the Scottish Government gave the green light for the beavers to remain.

Those championing the animals' return point to a boost to wildlife tourism, with visitors from all over the world visiting Knapdale and bringing economic benefits. There are also sizeable populations in Tayside and Perthshire and they are starting to spread further. Not everyone is happy. Some farmers and landowners regard them as pests, citing damage to trees and flooding in fields, and many animals have been shot. The Government has given the beaver protected status, but only time will tell how effective this is. You only need to look at the numerous deaths and disappearances of supposedly protected birds of prey to suspect this might not be the end of the struggle.

I looked at walking the trail at Knapdale, but my timing was constricted so it was unlikely I would catch sight of a beaver as they are most active at night. I reckoned the best I could hope for was some sign of activity, such as felled trees or stripped branches. Unfortunately, even this was to become a pipedream. One of my talks was moved back 12 hours, and, combined with days of heavy rain, the beaver expedition had to be ruled out altogether. If ever there was a time to say 'Ah gnaw' this was it.

We would just have to settle for seeing a dam, and it would have to be a man-made one. It seemed fitting then that we would be walking in the towering shadow of the Cruachan Dam. I don't wish to be disparaging about the work-rate and engineering skills of our aquatic rodent chums, but really, how can anyone compare this feat to those built with some gnawed trees and random sticks? I reckon the beavers are going to have to up their game if they are to assimilate properly into Scottish society.

§

THE storms that had defined September and October had finally blown away, leaving a period of calm ushered in on the back of a brief, but welcome, cold snap. The first snow always brings a frisson of excitement for mountain lovers, a taster menu for the joys they hope lie ahead. Winter is the season that teases us. It drags us through an emotional wringer. An early snow event followed by good consolidation and we are like children being handed the keys to a sweetie shop; a warmer winter of wind and rain, and we are cursing the gods of the north wind, praying for spring to arrive and put us out of our misery. Winter is the meteorological equivalent of having L-O-V-E and H-A-T-E tattooed on the hands.

A late-night journey north saw me sitting at the entrance to Strathfarrar, fidgeting while waiting for the clock to strike 9am and the gate to swing open. Only 25 cars are allowed in this glen at any one time, and in the summer there is often a queue. On this occasion, I needn't have worried – I was the only one waiting. The big attraction is the linked ridge of four Munros, but in the shorter hours of winter or under snow cover it's too big an undertaking. I had a more modest target, Beinn na Muice, a few hours at most. This rugged little hill provides views that would be the envy of many higher summits, in particular the one down the length of Loch Monar.

First light had revealed a good plastering of snow on the high tops, cover down to the road in places, the moon, now in a waxing gibbous phase, still holding its position past closing time. As I drove along the pitted road, flurries sprinted sporadically from invasive dark skies, juxtaposing with periods of bright sunshine which produced a landscape that glistened. The further down the glen I travelled, the deeper the snow I encountered. The ascent was in full winter kit, but the snow was soft, melting away with every footstep. In the three hours it took to circuit the hill, the lower landscape had returned to autumn, all blue skies, wispy white cloud and russet grasses, and a glen now populated by camera clubs.

The snowline had retreated further the following day, now just a gauze sheet laid over the higher reaches. I did find deeper pockets during the long ridge walk over to the distant of summit of Carn a' Choin Deirg in Glen Alladale, but it looked like this brief encounter with winter was already over. Despite the sunshine, there were a few chilly reminders that we were on the cusp of a change – frozen patches of water glittering, trapped grasses waving in formation, and an icy drop into a steep-sided glen bereft of light, bitter in the teeth of the wind funnelling through.

There were more idle threats of winter during an ascent of Carn an Tuirc in Glenshee to celebrate Hazel Strachan's latest Munro round 'compleation', flakes being driven across the slopes by a fierce wind, but without any real intent. The cold was enough to keep the celebrations short, Champagne now, cake later. Hazel's finishes have become an annual event, ones to be marked up on the calendar at the start of the year alongside the birthdays and family holidays. The turn-out seems to grow with each passing notch. Ten rounds in and she shows no sign of stopping: There's no telling what the final tally will be.

One week before the Cruachan walk, and it felt as though the year had started running in reverse. The occasional snow forays had surrendered and gone off to lick their wounds.

Now a high pressure system had taken control, bringing dry, clear, settled conditions, so I set off for a whistle-stop tour of the north-west. It always comes as a pleasant surprise to get the opportunity of three consecutive leisurely days on the hills at this time of year, and despite a busy schedule I had to take advantage.

I had been in Edinburgh the previous evening delivering a talk to a walking club, busy streets and jostling crowds at the rail station. Less than 12 hours later I was being held up by a duck roadblock near the cafe at Dalwhinnie. The non-flying pickets I could handle, city life less so. It reminded me why I had never regretted a minute of baling out of a well-paid, secure job, to spend my time in the outdoors.

The journey over the Bealach Ratagan and down into Glenelg merely reinforced my belief. Stripped trees punctuated swathes of gold and brown vegetation which rolled down from sweeping slopes of scree to reach the road, then continuing to the sparkling waters of Loch Hourn far below. A massive ray of sunlight burst the cloud cover, its spotlight focusing on a lone, bobbing boat on the loch, while Ladhar Bheinn remained a tall, dark and handsome presence in the background. It was a picture of autumnal serenity, perhaps too much so, because it brought with it a false sense of security.

I set off around midday to tackle the Druim Fada ridge. It's a track walk for an hour, a short steep climb, then a walk back along a grand highway of rocky lumps and bumps before dropping back down. Book time suggested around four and a half hours for the circuit, and I was confident I had a little time in hand. I reached the summit on schedule, a fine viewpoint to Knoydart where rogue rays of sunshine were lasering over Ladhar Bheinn and on to the waters of Loch Hourn.

It was a wrench to tear myself away but the consolation of the walk back were the metallic light shows from both sides of the ridge, silver to the left, copper to the right. It soon became obvious that the time and distance format used for working out the return journey may have added up on paper but didn't translate to reality. This was complex terrain, a series of stiff re-climbs and constant detours to find the best line. By the time I reached the final peak, I was around 30 minutes behind the supposed time.

The glowing patches on the side of Beinn Sgritheall and its acolytes told me I didn't have long before any remaining light vanished. I was about halfway down when the power was shut off completely. The ground was muddy and slippery, pitted with deep holes amid awkward tufts. It was difficult to predict what the next step held even with the torch; controlled stumbling was the order of the evening. The swiftness with which the dark had descended was alarming.

I set off next day in the cold darkness, but when the dawn started rising it came in fast and I was up and down Sgurr a' Gharaidh in four sunshine hours. A short drive over the Bealach na Ba pass to Applecross and I was ready to go again, this time up the long ridge of Beinn a' Chlachain. Again I started losing the light on the descent, but I had timed it well enough to make it down the steep and tricky slopes of heather and dead, brittle bracken without needing any artificial light, the sunset silhouettes of the Skye ranges on the horizon drawing me towards the finish line.

I left Torridon next morning in temperatures of 9C and watched the gauge nosedive to –4C during the run to Black Bridge. I knew this would be a long day but most of it was track walking. It was bitter at the start and I was walking in shadow for a long time in Strath Vaich, but the stunning contrast in autumnal light and shade conjured up a feeling of warmth. Ten hours later I was back at the car, a mere hour's worth of work for the torch, but vital all the same. It's unthinkable I could have taken a chance on any of these walks at this time of year without a torch. It's also a good thing that my reliance on the accuracy of book times has long faded. It pays to build in extra time as winter rolls in.

§

ANY hopes that the weather would stay clear and settled for the Beaver Moon walk were wiped away by the ferocity of the rain storms pushing in from the east. The most surprising element of the night walks so far had been the lack of rain. I had expected I would catch at least one night where I would be walking in constant rain, but so far the only precipitation had been the blizzards early in the year and a couple of hours of light rain on the way out from Ben Starav in August. I felt a soaking was overdue.

The good news for this outing was that the forecast was better the further west you were prepared to travel. I had to keep reminding myself of this as I drove through constant rain all the way to our meeting point in Tyndrum. The rain line should have been left behind by now.

Rachael appeared, then Rob and Katrina. It occurred to me that this had become a new phase in my life – meeting strangers in car parks at midnight all over the country. The moon showed for a bit, maybe didn't like what it saw, then ducked behind the clouds again. I could see it would be playing hard to get. There was still a touch of moisture in the air as we drove out to the starting point and a lively breeze that suggested we would face gusty conditions high on the ridge. The longer hours of darkness and the timing of the full moon meant the chances of catching spectacular views were remote. Sunset was too early and sunrise too late; this was simply a case of reaching the summit of Ben Cruachan and making it safely back down. If, by some miracle, it was clear up top, we were prepared to do a circuit of the ridge but no one was reckoning that as a possibility.

We went with full winter gear plus crampons and axes but within ten minutes of pushing upwards, layers were being stripped off. I began to wonder if I had miscalculated with heavy winter trousers. We had taken the simple route, through the rail underpass and then into the short stretch of tree cover but we quickly went astray, losing the path in the mounds of dead leaves and fallen branches. Rather than waste time searching, we stuck with our reading and found an alternative path over open ground that led us up to the hydro access road for a gentle stroll up to the dam. The moon broke through the cloud cover a few times, lighting the bare, high branches like witches' fingers, and filling us with a sense of optimism and possibility. It would be prove to be nothing more than taunting. We had started with head torches and they would remain on for the duration, no light relief in sight.

Our voices bounced around the massive ramparts of the dam, faint echoes in the otherwise silent night. Once up top, any illusion of light vanished. The cloud line smothered the ridge, no silhouetted spikes of this marvellous circuit of peaks on show. The water lay dormant, dark as obsidian, a random flash of white here and there to let us know of its presence. As we turned to make our way up to the col, there was a debate as to whether the whiteness on the slopes ahead was clinging mist or a covering of snow. The more we rose, the more obvious it became there was a patchy covering of white.

There's a motorway leading up here, not so much a path as a trench filled with rubble, but even with this obvious guideline every ounce of concentration was on foot placement. In darkness this deep, the torch provides only a narrow corridor of security and you have to fully focus on keeping your steps in the line of illumination. Stepping too wide can mean stepping into the unknown, on to loose rock or into a hole hidden in the darkness, easy to slip or stumble. The constant attentiveness can be tiring. It's one of the biggest differences from daylight walking, and Kat was beginning to notice. She said her legs were trembling, a sign of tiredness usually only felt on the way down near the end of a long day. There may have been a psychological factor at play, the feeling that you are struggling but not knowing the reason why. She improved almost instantly when informed that this was the result of the high levels of concentration being used up with every step.

We were greeted at the col by a blasting wind being channelled through the gap, but it eased as we turned north for the final steep push to the summit. The snow got deeper with every upward metre, the path invisible in places, the rocks of the boulder field rimed and slippery. Every step became awkward, a constant need to check the lie of the land before committing to the next step. It's easy to turn an ankle in this terrain. The great advantage of steep ascents is that they tend to be short-lived and we were soon standing at the sawn-off trig pillar. There was little to see, the slopes falling away on all sides disappearing into the blackness, the ridge ahead invisible. There was no point in hanging around. The wind was whipping over the summit, loose straps smacking into the side of the face.

The gang lined up for a summit photo, proof we had been there. The night vision picked up every minuscule drop of moisture blowing in the wind and made it seem like we were in a white-out. It looked impressive, if not entirely truthful, but at least the smiles on the faces were genuine. It may not have been the best conditions for a night walk, but reaching the summit in these relatively alien circumstances could be considered reward in itself.

I was disappointed for Rob and Kat. Any hope they had of a photoshoot to use in the magazine had been blown away. They had chosen to come out on the darkest night and it hadn't worked out. Had they been out on the May or June walks they would have had an entirely different experience.

Rachael was an old hand at this night walking lark, having climbed in Europe, Africa and the Himalayas. She had also walked with me at night at the Arran Mountain Festival during even more trying weather conditions than we were facing on Cruachan, and with much less experienced companions. Her navigation skills on that wet and windy night in the hills had proved invaluable.

Many regard New Zealand as the Scotland of the southern hemisphere, its mountains and unpredictable climate a mirror of our own, so it's no surprise to learn that Rachael regards this country as her second home. She certainly has the credentials; her red hair, work ethic and spirit of adventure testimony to her Scottish heritage, grandparents who left these shores long ago. The travel bug is also inherent, years of listening to tales of her parents' excursions around the globe.

Scotland is the latest stop in her journey and she admits to being fortunate to be able to work doing what she loves. A mountain leader and climbing instructor, she has also worked with the Mountains and the People project, learning how to build and restore paths. I was interested to hear how she felt the two countries' landscapes compared, and also where she saw differences. She loves her homeland and can see many similarities with the mountains in Scotland, but she reckons there is no other landscape in the world like ours.

She loves the sheer expanse of our mountain landscape, the

fact you can be just an hour from the car yet be staring out at an expanse of white-capped peaks, the feeling of being in a mountain range which feels as though it spans hundreds of miles, wild and beautiful. She's a big fan of Scottish winters and loves the fact there's so much ancient evidence of the forces of nature.

"I love when the first snow arrives and the days have that dusky blue light, the colour of the lochs is almost black, the birch trees have lost their leaves and they turn the hillsides a shade of mauve, the hill slopes threaded with bands of gold from the dead bracken contrasted against the white of the snow capping the tops. It's such a special experience.

"I remember the first time I stood on Ben Macdui taking in that view into the Lairig Ghru, that perfectly formed U-shaped valley, and trying to comprehend the power behind its formation. New Zealand is a younger landscape. Those glacial valleys are still full of ice, and the forces forming the mountains are still all too often felt right under your feet."

She feels we are blessed with our outdoor access laws. They are the envy of the world, and Rachael wishes her homeland would follow our lead. There is protection for strips of land around most rivers, lakes and the coastline, and in the national parks, but private ownership of land and the question of access is still a big problem. The major difference, however, is that the treeline in New Zealand is much higher and the mountains are extensively covered in forest. You can't just walk wherever you choose as you can here, you have to use cut tracks as the forest is too dense.

Openness in our landscape is one thing, but the dearth of tree cover is a serious cause for concern. The ancient Caledonian Forest was estimated to have covered more than 3.5 million acres, a vast wilderness of Scots pine, birch, rowan, aspen, oak and juniper. It was home to bears, wolves, beaver, boar and many other species. Birds and insects were in abundance. A long history of deforestation has reduced it to small struggling pockets, disconnected fragments often filled with dead and dying trees and little new growth.

Recurring floods and landslides have shown that denuded slopes are no match for heavy rainfall. Bald may be beautiful in some people's eyes, but not when thousands of tons of mud are thundering down unchecked. Meanwhile, the grouse moors stretch on unchallenged, barren landscapes for the shooting set to blast away the remaining wildlife and woe betide any hare that pops its head above the heather, while birds of prey continue to mysteriously disappear in our avian Bermuda Triangle.

The best hill days are often those which have an approach through mixed woodland, a gentle introduction to the rigours of the day ahead with birdsong, butterflies and wild flowers.

Glen Affric still delights despite not being fully recovered from the recent assaults by heavy machinery, and the reinforcement of the straggling Crannach Wood at the foot of Beinn Achaladair and Beinn a' Chreachain is encouraging. There are many other signs that the tide is turning, but it does seem incredible it hasn't happened long before now considering the posturing of politicians of all hues over environmental concerns.

The extra factor that confirmed Rachael as a perfect partner for this night project was that she had climbed the 'real' Mountains of the Moon, the Rwenzori in eastern equatorial Africa. These glaciated, rocky peaks are the continent's highest range, sprawling over the border between Uganda and the Democratic Republic of the Congo. Rwenzori is a local name which means 'rain-maker'. It's easy to sympathise – every mountain in Scotland could fall under that umbrella. They were first referred to as the Mountains of the Moon by the Greek astronomer Ptolemy around 1800 years ago when he predicted that an unknown range of mountains in this area were the likely source of the Nile. Their existence was brought to wider attention in 1888 by the explorer Henry Stanley, after whom the highest mountain, Mount Stanley, is named. It rises to a height of 5,109 metres on its main summit, Margherita Peak.

The attraction of a mountain range sitting almost on top of the equator is obvious for someone so interested in botany. It's one of the most biodiverse places on the planet, the conditions perfect for a riot of colourful plant life, including heathers that reach 30 metres. Remember that the next time you complain about hacking your way through chest-high bracken.

The preparations were intense, the potential hazards many; altitude sickness, malaria, floods and huge electrical storms, and the occasional passing cobra. The upside – no midges. Perhaps surprisingly, the moon was an infrequent visitor. The position of the mountains on the equator mean the moon and sun rise and set almost instantly, no drawn-out sunsets or sunrises as in the northern or southern hemispheres.

I didn't feel so guilty about the lack of a moon on our walk now. Rachael was a kindred spirit, another supporter to the joys of the sensory experience of walking in darkness, where sound replaces sight as the primary receptor, where the imagination can be given full reign. She told of crossing glaciers in the middle of the night, looking down into the pitch-black, unfathomable depths of crevasses, while thunder rocked the angry skies above. This is nature writ large, and there's a realisation we are privileged to be participants in something over which we have no control.

Our descent from the summit of Ben Cruachan was uneventful, no altitude sickness, no snakes. We made our way down carefully through the boulders, at one point catching a few hefty sideswipes from a sudden and scouring wind which made it hard to stand but it seemed to be constrained to an a few metres and we soon left it behind. I must admit to a huge sigh of relief that this one proved so lacking in drama; any walk in late November is in the lap of the gods and there was always the nagging doubt that this could be the one where I came undone.

We had stayed dry, and were just in time to be chapping at the door for a well-earned breakfast in Tyndrum. My eyes had already turned north for the final moon of the year, the Cold Moon, and the summit of Ben Hope on December 22.

One final note. The following day I was contacted by someone who said he had spotted our lights rising steadily on Ben Cruachan around 2am. It seems you can't even sneak up a remote mountain these days without being detected.

13
Days of Hope

COLD MOON

(Saturday, December 22, 17.48)
Mountain: *Ben Hope*
Soundtrack: *Great High Mountain – Jack White*
Celebratory drink: *Modus Hoperandi pale ale*

Ben Hope, December 22. The first night after the winter solstice on the most northerly Munro for the 13th and final full moon of the year: The Cold Moon. It was a description that could fit readily to any mountain in the country at this time of year, but I had always thought it appropriate to finish the year on hope. I also believed it may not be possible to live up to that expectation.

The chances of a perfect night would be slimmer than usual. I would happily have settled for making the short push to the summit and down again in anything less than horrendous conditions. In the end, Hope prevailed. It may have been only a fleeting encounter with the Cold Moon, but the timing could not have been better.

I had learned early it was better to have at least one option for every planned full moon walk. Sometimes the links would be obvious, sometimes they might require a bit of left-field thinking. Ben Hope was the exception. It was the first mountain to be pencilled in at the start of the project, and it was the one I was least prepared to sacrifice. Barring another Beast from the East or any other direction, I would just grin and bear whatever the skies could throw at me. After all, I had survived blizzards and white-outs, I had survived storms and gale-force winds. I was confident there would be a grand finale. But the nearer I got to the finishing line, the more the doubts started to niggle in the back of my mind. All or nothing is never a great situation. I couldn't afford a massive anti-climax, and the only way to insure against that was to have a realistic Plan B.

Ben Hope is a solitary mountain and it's a long way off, so this would not be an overnight trip. I needed to give myself as much breathing space as possible. This required finding a base for a few days in the far north of Scotland in late December. Just before Christmas. It's a sparsely served area at the best of times, and at this time of year most of the hotels, pubs, restaurants and lodgings had closed their doors until spring.

There were two possibilities, the hostels at Durness and Tongue. Both were open, both were within easy striking distance of the mountain. It seemed a simple enough task; contact both and see if they had any bed spaces. I should have checked the Laws of Simplicity, particularly No.9: Some things can never be made simple.

I emailed both and got one reply within an hour informing me there were rooms available. I didn't hesitate. I gave my details and paid the deposit. The name on the reply was Mackay, and I knew that the owners of the Durness hostel were called Mackay, so Durness it was. Except, it wasn't. Next morning I got another reply, again from someone named Mackay. I assumed this was a follow-up call from another member of staff and told them I had already booked with someone called Carol. No one here by that name, I was told. My first thought then was that I had been the victim of a scam. It took a bit of to-ing and fro-ing before it became obvious that I had actually booked with the hostel at Tongue. It seems everyone up here is the real Mackay.

Confusion over and base camp established, I turned my attention to the possible doomsday scenario of what would happen if I couldn't even reach Tongue because of blocked or closed roads. The fact that Storm Deirdre was trying its best to rip the roof off my house at that very moment probably helped concentrate the mind. Then it came to me: If I couldn't reach the most northerly Munro, I could do a complete volte-face and go for the most southerly. Ben Lomond means 'beacon hill', so it could be described that I would be finishing on a beacon of hope. As soon as I had worked that out, I knew nothing would stop me reaching the summit of Ben Hope. It's only when you have no choice that things tend to go pear-shaped.

The final walk had attracted a bit of attention. Three fellow members from my mountain club, Pauline, Joan and Andy, wanted to join me for the last summit. I was touched that they were willing to travel all the way from Dundee for the occasion.

Katrina from *The Scots Magazine* was also keen to come along. It would be a good chance for her to get some pictures for the article they were running, especially as the Beaver Moon walk the previous month had been so disappointing. Besides, this would be a new Munro for her, but I'm sure that thought never crossed her mind. The BBC had also been in touch to arrange a radio piece for their *Out For the Weekend* programme. Live from Tongue – it's not often you can make that boast.

Then there was Eileen, a university lecturer in Glasgow. Eileen had first made contact about a year earlier. She was working on a professional doctorate in psychology and had been intrigued by the premise of my first book, *Moonwalker*, and how I had managed to juggle being a journalist by day and a mountain walker by night. She wanted to understand what key characteristics had provided the psychological resilience to keep life and work in balance, the ability to survive and thrive through this transformation from a shackled desk job with unsociable hours and stressful deadlines to the physical and psychological freedom of the hills.

There was also a personal interest. Eileen felt she was in need of a similar transformation, so she was keen to meet someone who had been down that road. We recorded a podcast in March in which we discussed the trials and tribulations of those 15 years of night walking. Being a keen hillwalker and having 162 Munros under her belt, she could relate to the joys and struggles of walking in the Scottish mountains. She felt the time was right to experience a night walk. I mentioned I was working on a third book, *Mountains of the Moon*, and would welcome company on any of the walks. Besides, I was keen to delve deeper into the psychological factors that had been a feature in driving me on to this mountain path for so many years.

The idea of Ben Hope in December provided the perfect opportunity to answer her question: what psychological and physical traits do you need to climb a Munro in the dark and in the middle of winter?

This completed the circle. I now had my modus operandi for the big finish. Equally importantly, I also had a few cans of a beer called Modus Hoperandi for the apres climb celebration. Even the weather was playing ball. The storms had cleared through and the forecast held no nasty surprises, possible light snow on the high tops, light winds, and a good chance of clear nights. A zen-like calm had settled in after the anxieties of the previous couple of ascents. I felt I could relax and enjoy the ride.

Ben Hope has always held a special magnetism for mountaineers. Now it felt as if we were all being drawn north.

§

I'M still climbing upward and my journey's almost ended. A line from the song Great High Mountain, a piece of music that had been stuck in my head for months. It's a traditional slice of Americana reworked by Jack White for the soundtrack of the film, *Cold Mountain*. The music is no hurry to go anywhere, a slow, haunting lament prodded along by languid fiddles, melancholy and yet joyful at the same time. The lyrics are ostensibly about faith, the culmination of a great journey after a long, uphill struggle a metaphor for life. They resonated with me on a much simpler level, references such as the need to climb and the view from the top. This was the perfect piece to close the concert, a chill-out soundtrack on the long drive to climb a stand-out mountain.

The song was still echoing in my head as I picked Eileen up from the train station at Inverness. It had been an undemanding run up the A9, the benign conditions adding to the relaxed feel of the trip. We still had a few hours to go to reach Tongue, plenty time to reflect on the challenges thrown up during the previous 11 months of the challenge.

The chat was relaxed; I was being interviewed without realising it. Eileen's ability to tease out responses was a testament to the experience of her thesis work, where listening is not just about hearing the content of the conversation but also about picking up on the emotions between the lines. She homed in on the mental agility she believed was needed to remain resilient when undertaking a challenge over a prolonged period, picking up on the passion and the energy involved, not only the physical and psychological input but also the heart and soul.

I was impressed to hear of the training regime Eileen had undertaken since committing to the walk. She had changed her running to a night schedule to become more familiar with exercising with a head torch. She also took part in the National Three Peaks Challenge and climbed 20 Munros. During a summer hiatus in the USA, she walked parts of the Appalachian Trail, climbed Mount Washington and went open water swimming regularly. She ran and did aerobics every day to increase strength and endurance. She also focused heavily on diet by adding two micro-nutrient drinks to her menu each day; a blend of lemon, lime, ginger, garlic and mineral water first thing, then later a mix of kale, spinach, avocado, cucumber, broccoli and broccoli sprout. I was beginning to think I had stumbled on to the secret identity of Wonder Woman. I wouldn't learn the real reason for this intensive regime until later.

We dropped into Lairg and a sea of mist which had spilled over from the surface of Loch Shin, giving the surrounding streets the eerie stillness of a ghost town. We drifted out the other side to clarity and the split in the road which offers two single-track options that form a giant horseshoe to the north coast and then back round. We went right. We passed through a deserted landscape of burnt browns, land that looked as though it was waiting for the overdue winter to come calling. Ben Klibreck had a curious, precariously-placed yet static cloud bonnet, darker slopes rising from russet foundations, just the odd rib of white standing out. We pushed through Altnaharra, the only place to challenge Braemar on record cold temperatures, then passed a sign on the left indicating the minor road cutting round to Ben Hope.

The low-lying sun was spilling its light over the waters of Loch Loyal and Loch Craggie. There was the merest hint of Ben Hope off to our left but the scene was dominated by the crags and towers of Ben Loyal. Its ramparts would remain by our side for the remainder of the drive. It changed constantly, a waterfall of cloud tumbling between the summits as if feeling its way around the contours, rolling over the edge but never quite falling, the visibility shifting with every wave.

The high part of Tongue seemed to be a mix of cottage ruins and holiday houses, each with the same empty outcome, signs of life only starting to appear at the bottom of the dramatic switchback which leads down to the water's edge and the causeway over the Kyle of Tongue. The last time I had been up here had been in summer and the contrast was stark. Then it was all greens and blues, mountain faces lit pale by the sun, busier roads and plenty of people around. Now it felt like somewhere at the edge of the world, translucent waters overseen by bubbling skies and a weakening sun, the hills dark shapes on the periphery, brooding and unpredictable, and there didn't seem to be another soul around. I began to wonder if I had just dreamt being here before.

The hostel sits right at the eastern end of the causeway, but we weren't expected until later so decided to drive round to the foot of Ben Hope to check out some of the logistics involved for the walk and try to get an idea of conditions on the hill. The road through Strath More is rough and narrow with a grass Mohican running up the centre but the landscape is one to savour. Finding the start point for some walks is sometimes the biggest problem, but even the most navigationally challenged will be okay here. A big sign – Way up, Ben Hope – points out the route. There was one other car parked and a pair of walkers were just arriving back as we pulled in. They were able to give us a report on conditions higher up, and they seemed slightly incredulous when we told them we were going up at night. They were from the Inverness area, so this was a day outing for them. As usual, once we got chatting, they came round to the idea that it wasn't madness, just different. The night fell like a guillotine, an all-enveloping blackness with little warning, our headlights now the only breach for miles. An icy chill had also descended. The drive back was enlivened by golden plovers in kamikaze mode, swooping and diving out from the trees into the grass in the centre of the road, a late insect supper before lights out. They were perched on every boulder along both sides of the road, voicing their impatience, waiting for their chance.

We were grateful for the warm welcome at the hostel, despite being the only occupants. A former hunting lodge, this has the feeling of a grand old house, all polished wood and big lazy furniture and a blazing open fire. There's also a well-stocked in-house shop, complete with choice of wine, beer and ciders, everything you need to be cut off from the outside world for a week or two.

I had been toying with the idea of going up Ben Hope the night before the full moon walk to reacquaint myself with the route and look out for any potential problems. The forecast wasn't the best, so I suggested to Eileen we go the next morning instead. It would let us start off in the dark and hopefully walk into a sunrise.

Porridge and coffee at 6am and then we set off in icy darkness. The single-track road along the side of Loch Hope was brilliant white, as though encrusted with millions of tiny diamonds sparkling under the lights. We were greeted with a biting cold as we exited the car and carried out the final checks on our gear. You can never have too many checks, especially when setting off under cover of darkness. We had already double checked everything at the hostel before setting off, but now we did another rundown and swept the area with our torches to make sure nothing had fallen out on the ground or was left hanging from the car.

Years of night walking had made this second nature for me, but for Eileen this was a new and vital learning curve. She said she had immediately detected a heightening in her senses, and was grateful for the additional verbal safety checklist. She said it gave her an early confidence boost, not only in the success of the challenge but in the emotional intelligence required for a successful and pleasurable climb.

We set off uphill on the path by invisible, whispering waters. The chill vanished quickly and it wasn't long before we were removing layers. The atmospherics were curious. It seemed as if the country was split evenly in half, and we were right on the border. Everything to the west was duller and cloud-capped, while to the east there was more clarity and a crisper feel. As if to prove the point, a fine drizzle began to sweep in as we rose, but it stopped abruptly as though hitting an invisible barrier.

It didn't need much height to encounter patches of brittle ground, and the last few hundred metres were in a deep freeze, grasses bowed in suspended animation, rocks coated thickly with rime and ice blast, but there was never any need for crampons or even an ice axe. Just before the final rise there is a jumble of ice-blasted rocks sticking out in all directions that bring to a mind a neglected cluster of tombstones. It lends a slightly eerie feel to proceedings, especially under this chilly, white veil. The summit trig point sat like an ice queen on a throne of white stones, the views beyond hidden by a circuit of grey despite hints of blue sky circling far above. The sunrise remained unseen, the switch from night to day muted, almost imperceptible.

I had been carrying out a running commentary during the climb at the request of BBC Scotland. During a call the previous evening to confirm the timings for the *Out For the Weekend* interview later next day, they had asked if I would be able to provide an audio recording to be used for a short segment on their Saturday morning show, *Out of Doors*. It seemed I was destined to be ruling the airwaves that weekend.

Eileen, meanwhile, took a few moments at the summit to say a prayer for a friend's father, a fellow Munro bagger and all-round adventurer, who had recently passed away. She had brought his order of service to the top of the mountain, a tribute to a man well-loved and a life well lived.

We took the long way round on our return, past the Dun Dornaigil broch and back out over the weather Maginot Line into brilliant sunshine and glistening waters. Ben Klibreck's cloud cap had slipped off, its bulk now acting as a giant sunscreen. We passed a lone, abandoned house, guarded by a pair of skeletal trees, and with Ben Loyal as a prime site backdrop. It's hard to imagine the struggle that must have been involved living here. The perspective is so shatteringly different; many would see it as a romantic beauty spot, the occupants as a refuge from a harsh and unforgiving existence.

We arrived back at the hostel to be greeted by Pauline and Andy. Joan, the third member of the party, had called off ill but she had sent a home-made curry. We retired to the lounge and sank into the sofas to enjoy the blazing fire, alongside a party of local ladies who had been in for Christmas dinner. Their conversation turned to the pros and cons of the Space Hub being planned nearby at The Moine on the north coast, which would be used for commercial satellite and rocket launches. The arguments were age-old and there was no consensus; some saw it as a possibility to help the community and boost a dwindling population, others were more cynical, seeing it as more unwanted development that would only go into the pockets of a select few.

Radio time was approaching, time to get the Tongue wagging. I was given the freedom and privacy of the office to wait for the call, and then was played in with The Waterboys number, The Whole of the Moon. Presenter Fiona Stalker was in her usual excellent form and kept the chat flowing smoothly, from the choices of the mountains and the moons, to the music and the drinks. The others had gone outside to sit in their cars to listen to the broadcast, a concession to non-interference. Then it was radio silence in Tongue again. It had felt like a long day, and we now had 24 hours to wait for the final ascent. It was time to chill.

Eileen had gone to the trouble of producing a steak pie for the evening meal with the words Ben Hope carved into the pastry, and a separate string of letters on the plate spelling Moonwalker. I have eaten many pies in my 64 years on this earth but never before had I had one specially baked in my honour.

§

THE big day dawned. We were up and about early, Eileen off running across the causeway, Pauline, Andy and myself down on the shore hoping to catch a sunrise. A brief flash of pink and yellow on the eastern horizon raised our hopes, but it proved to be something of a false dawn and the morning settled lazily back into a pewter palette, a typical winter torpor, the only sound the rhythmic lapping of the water on the rocky shoreline.

We spotted a seal's head breaching the surface, a lone hunter in the gloom, and there was plenty evidence that this was an otter hotspot, at least for the toilet facilities. Ben Loyal's serrated skyline was crystal clear, but the cloud was stacking up on the top end of Ben Hope. Off to the east, the clouds had taken on a pinkish tinge, reflecting in the brighter and calmer waters on the other side of the barrier.

We retreated to the hostel for breakfast. There were restful periods and there were casual walks around the village, but the day was all about anticipation, waiting for the sunlight to vacate its short shift. We finally set off just after 2pm, Loch Hope a silver blade shimmering under a massive central parting in the cloud cover. Kat was waiting for us when we arrived. The temperature had risen but the chances of a clear night had fallen. We met a walker coming down with his dog. He was in full winter solstice mode, having climbed Ben Klibreck in the morning to try to catch the sunrise, then Ben Hope for the sunset and now he was off to Ben Loyal for the full moon. We wished him better luck third time out.

We made our way up in a disappointing drizzle, the cloud and mist blocking out the stars and the route ahead. The moon was nowhere to be seen, not even a hint of a faint light. It was only another walk up a mountain but this was supposed to be the grand finale to a year which had started with full moon walks in blizzards and white-outs, before calming to a run of achingly beautiful sunrises and sunsets, and then plunging back into high winds and seemingly endless hours of darkness.

Strange the thoughts that pass through your head at times like these, the places you look for inspiration, the places you look for hope. The words of Martin Luther King seemed fitting: Carve a tunnel of hope through the dark mountain of disappointment. We certainly had the dark mountain and we were carving our tunnel steadily upwards in the gloom. This was the simple route up, a wide ramp rising at an easy angle on a motorway path. When you see shots of the mountain from overhead, a different beast is revealed. That easy access route is squeezed between a horseshoe of steep flanks on the west, north, and east. The north-west face in particular is the domain of the climber. Walkers can tackle the mountain from the north, but most will choose to avoid the exposed scramble up an intimidating rock step and take the easier gully to the left. There are also possible routes to the east to the twin lochans, and but in tricky weather conditions or bad visibility the south ridge is always the surest line. We were happy to stick with this uncomplicated run to the finish line.

Then, as we started the push up the final rise, we caught a faint glow in the sky. At last. This was the Cold Moon, trying to push its way through the clouds. We stopped to watch, silently cheering it on, but it seemed the battle was being lost. For five minutes we stood, scared to move off in case the moon would emerge triumphant for a few seconds and we would miss it.

Our vigil paid off. One mighty thrust and it was there in all its glory, concentric rainbow rings pulsating. It stood its ground, resolute for the next half hour, accompanying us up the ridge, until the cloud, now regrouped, swept in to smother the light again. We were disappointed, but given the earlier conditions, were happy to accept small mercies.

We continued along the ever flattening terrain leaving imprints in the freshly falling snow until the faint outline of the summit trig point could be seen dead ahead in the mist. We approached with a noble silence which occurred organically. No chatter, no rustling of gear, not even a sound from our footsteps. The stillness and the silence were incredibly powerful, a true feeling of serenity.

Fifty steps to the finish ... 40 ... 30 ... 20 ... and then the unexpected twist in the tale as the clouds parted and the Cold Moon exploded back on to the scene, a superhero back from the dead in the nick of time. From zero visibility seconds before we now had 360-degree vision, the distant lights of remote buildings twinkling far below, the outlines of surrounding ridges and rock formations standing out. The lunar light cast on the string of lochans dropping down through the blackness in stages looked like golden teardrops, as if the moon itself were weeping with joy.

As a child of July, I had been interested to learn that the full moon was in Cancer, a sign that the evening would be one of sensitivity and emotion. I had expected to feel more emotion, but relief was the greatest one. I was still aware of the importance of not dropping my guard until we were back down safely. Eileen, however, told me later she had observed a change in my demeanour. She felt my posture had changed, that I seemed to grow a few inches and that even my brow had unfurrowed.

We drank in as much as we could of the moment, aware it wasn't going to last. There was a different darkness rumbling in from the north, boiling and threatening, and within the blink of an eye we were engulfed. We followed our footsteps in the snow and dropped fast. We were in a blackout and went offline for a few minutes, but that was mainly for safety reasons, and we soon regained the path. We made one stop at a large marker cairn to take on some sustenance and apart from some tentative steps down the wet rocks near the bottom, we all made it back in one piece. The spirit of hope had endured. Maybe I had made it on to the right side of Santa's list after all.

We broke open the beers on our return, before moving on to Champers and more curry than we could handle in the dining room. The emotion was more evident now. I felt drained, as if the whole year had suddenly come crashing into the party. It took all the energy I had left to pull myself out of the deep easy chair and away from that roaring fire and retire for the night.

It was a long road home, but for the first time in months I felt a weight had been lifted from my shoulders. I was tired but there was a mix of satisfaction and relief. Now I could relax and enjoy the festive period with the family, no more night mountain planning, no more thinking about the timing of the moons.

There was one last surprise, however. As the conversation flowed with reflective learnings, Eileen told me that she had been recently been diagnosed with multiple sclerosis and that her vision had been reduced by 65 per cent. She had spent the last couple of months agonising over whether to go ahead with the walk, mainly because she was worried there was a danger she might spoil my big moment by having to turn back on the mountain. Instead, she responded in the most positive way possible, working as hard as she could to ensure her fitness. Suddenly the whole intense build-up to climb one Munro made perfect sense. She wanted to make sure that the parts of her body that did work were at the optimum level.

She told me it had been a hard year, but climbing Ben Hope was a tonic. It had given her a purpose through the darkness. The recce climb had given her the confidence to meet the challenge head on.

She had come along primarily to study my psychological and physical resilience but instead had discovered her own. She had followed the premise that human life is fleeting; you can blink and it's over, but living it is truly worth it.

Maybe I had been to the top of a mountain with Wonder Woman. It was a fine way to end an epic year.

Mountains of the Moon

Bonus track*: The Whole of the Moon – The Waterboys*

When I was at primary school, we were given a home project which involved taking pieces of felt and stitching them together to make an animal. There were two choices – a mouse or an elephant. The mouse was three small pieces of similar length to be joined up and stuffed with foam, then a couple of little ears and a tail to be attached. The elephant was about four times the size and involved more stitching on more sections of a bigger body, plus four legs and a trunk to be sewn and filled separately.

The mouse was the easier choice for those who didn't know the first thing about needlecraft. Having never stitched or sewn anything before, my decision was obvious. I arrived home and told my mum about my homework.

She said with a sigh: "And I'll bet you chose the bloody elephant."

For the next few weeks it was literally the elephant in the room. Needless to say, it was my overworked mum who spent hours sewing together a green jumbo and then packing it with foam.

I was seven years old, but even at this tender age I reckon this could be read as a metaphor for the rest of my life. Whenever there's a choice, I have tended to plump for the elephant over the mouse.

That stuffed elephant came to mind a few times during my year of full moon walks. Those were the times when I was battling blizzards and gale-force winds to reach my target mountain when I could have taken an easier option. But I had laid out a set of rules at the outset, and I was determined I should play by those rules, no matter what.

Taken in sporting terms, the final table read:

Played 13, Won 10, Drawn 2, Lost 1.

Probably a B+ on my report card. Or as Meat Loaf might have put it had he shown more ambition in his numeracy skills: Twelve out of thirteen ain't bad.

It was impressive considering the restrictions. Picking 13 high mountain walks on 13 specific nights in our rogue climate was always going to be a lucky dip. I had fully expected to be battling the elements more often than not. There were options for extreme weather, but the parameters were narrow. I knew it was likely I would lose at least two or three of the walks, but only one fell, the Worm Moon, and that was down to the so-called Beast from the East rendering the roads impassable. Had I been thinking ahead, I could have saved that one by setting off west a few days earlier while travel was still possible and where mountain conditions were not so severe. Lessons were learned from that debacle. Indeed, the whole year turned out to be a constant learning curve.

At times, 2018 felt like it was going on forever, yet in other respects it whizzed past. There were times when I felt like pulling the plug. The early walks on Beinn Alligin and Cairn Gorm were particularly challenging. Then there was the lost one, before an unexpectedly intimidating night on Bla Bheinn. That felt like the last straw. Well, the second to last straw. I decided to give it one more shot, more in hope than expectation.

I had been writing the book as I had been going along, but I began to feel there was an element of tempting fate and after this misadventure I put the writing on hold. The whole idea was starting to feel bonkers. I would pick up again when – and if – I finished.

Beinn Eighe in late April for the Strawberry Moon was the turning point. The next three were spectacular, the rewards of a long, hot summer, and the August paddle over the glassy waters of Loch Etive to Ben Starav went to plan. I had broken the back of the project. Even if I had to shorten or adjust some of the remaining walks, I was going to finish. The September and October walks were a return to shorter daylight hours and were wind-battered affairs. November on Ben Cruachan was the darkest, so black that even Eric Olthwaite would have been impressed. It was also the one that made me feel most nervous. The end was so close, I began to think it was inevitable I would break an ankle or incur some other injury just inches from the finish line. I knew that once this one was over, I could relax and enjoy the planning for Ben Hope.

I got lucky. On any other year in recent times, I would have struggled. We had an exceptional late spring and that rolled on through the summer. Autumn was stormy but there was enough leeway and good light. The first snows of early winter came and went briefly, leaving relatively benign conditions for that time of year. Normally when it's man v the elements, I would always take the elements for an away win. Not this time.

The biggest surprise was the lack of rain. I had expected to have a couple of dank nights trudging round in constant misery, soaked to the skin, feet trying their best to swim along in the lochs forming in my boots. But we were eight months in before I felt the pitter-patter, two hours of annoying light precipitation along the shore of Loch Etive in the pre-dawn gloom after the long night on Ben Starav. There were also drizzly interludes on the October and December walks, but nothing to email home about.

The wind was the most consistent nuisance factor. It kept me from getting to the summits of Beinn Alligin and Cairn Gorm, brought a feel of winter chill on an autumn night on Beinn a' Ghlo, and had us crawling up to the summit plateau of Lochnagar.

I also got lucky with the midges. There was a brief encounter on the Loch Hourn road at midnight, but once I started gaining height, they were left behind.

I managed to cover most of the main mountain areas; Cairngorms, Torridon, Skye, Affric, Knoydart – or at least the Rough Bounds – Etive, Sutherland, but inevitably there were some great peaks that never made the cut. The biggest regret was that I didn't manage to fit in a visit to An Teallach. It's on the moonlight to-do list, though.

Ben Nevis was another notable absentee, as was Ladhar Bheinn and Ben More on Mull, but neither really slotted together neatly with the profile of the moons. I reluctantly decided to leave out Buachaille Etive Mor as I have watched the sunrise from the summit of Stob Dearg on more than one occasion. The loss of the remote A' Mhaighdean was also regrettable but necessary for safety reasons. I was able to console myself with the fact that I had recently sat at its summit for two hours watching the sun take its time to sink below the horizon, and then walked out over the rest of the Fisherfield fraternity in the burning oranges and reds of dawn.

Still, it leaves plenty of food for thought in the nights ahead.

§

IT had been nearly ten years since I had walked regularly in the mountains at night. When I started, it had been born of what I saw as necessity, a need to get around the problem of anti-social working hours, and an antidote to the stresses of the job. It fitted in with my lifestyle, and I became used to the irregular hours. I still love going out at night. The difference is that I can pick and choose my moments.

Setting myself a target of walking a Munro on every full moon was like stepping back in time to those 15 years of regular night walking. In fact, it would be harder. In those days, I could pick and choose the best weather, the days when I was least tired.

I'm ten years older now, if not ten years wiser. The knees have ten years more wear and tear on them, the eyes ten years' further deterioration. I would be going against regular sleep patterns as opposed to when they were more streamlined with my working hours. A strict commitment to a certain mountain at a certain time would be tough. There were times in the past when I had planned to go out, but by the time the end of the shift rolled round, I was too tired to make the effort and I would leave it for another day, or night. I couldn't do that now. Everything would be in the moment or not at all. The full moon was there and then it was gone. You couldn't play catch up. A few years back while delivering a talk, I was asked if I always chose to go out on nights with a full moon. The answer was 'No'. I went with the weather rather than the lunar schedule. But I wonder if that was when the seed for the full moon project had been planted.

The one advantage I had was experience. I had climbed around 300 mountains at night, including many on the 2018 schedule. I knew the routes, I knew the potential hazard points, I knew the escape routes. I also had a maturity that comes with many years walking the mountains. The need to simply reach the summits had been left behind long ago.

The timing was fortuitous. I had been looking at the full moon schedule a year earlier, unaware of the significance of the cycles of 2018, the 13 full moons which included a Blue Moon x two. It was a once in a generation opportunity. I couldn't wait. Things started moving fast, so fast that I didn't really have much time to think. I was heading up Beinn Alligin before the Bells had stopped. It was exciting.

It didn't take long for that excitement to wear thin. I had envisaged walking along sparkling snow ridges under a carpet of stars, the moon's light picking out every contour, the silence only breached by the crunch of my footsteps. The reality was different. This was tough going, a constant struggle upwards burdened by a weighty pack, in driving snow and limited visibility.

There was an intensity to these walks. There was no time for relaxation. I would spend weeks of anxiety building up to each one, eyes constantly on the weather. The forecasts this far in advance are unreliable, but the merest suggestion of good conditions would give me optimism, while a double raindrop would be a symbolic gesture of worry. The logistics would change like the weather, day by day.

It was worse when others were involved. I had company on seven of the 13 walks, and I appreciated the efforts made in every case. But I have a problem walking with others when I am the organiser – I feel it's my responsibility to make sure everyone has an enjoyable experience, and guilty if the walk is less than perfect. It's probably why I am happier being out on my own.

Everyone who came out said they found it a unique experience; some loved it, some endured it; some couldn't wait to do it again, while once was enough for others. It's similar to the introduction to any activity. If the first experience is a good one, you can get hooked. If it's not so good, you can be put off for life.

The result of all this angst was a fraught build-up to each outing. I found it hard to sleep, the night walks intruding on my hours of supposed repose. Sometimes, I would hear the black dog barking. Once the day arrived, all the troubles were overcome by the pure joy of being out on the hill. The mind was able to escape from its tension-filled prison and rejoice in the spirit of freedom, the body boosted by the physical effort which would overtake the mental strain. No sooner had one walk been successfully completed, than that brief moment of euphoria or relief would be replaced by my mind leaping ahead to the next on the list, and the cycle would begin again.

I had often wondered just where my head went on its holidays. Now I knew. I may have had regrets at points and there were times when I questioned just what the hell I was doing being out in the mountains on certain nights. It was so different from my previous night walk experiences. It was tough physically, but the mental side was far tougher. I hadn't fully realised the toll the commitment to such a rigid programme would take out of me.

Age obviously played a big part. I was surprised to discover just how dark it often was, and how I often I needed the use of the head torch, a complete contrast from earlier nights when I could walk round a chain of hills without even taking it out of the bag. Some nights it just seemed like a slog, a means to an end, and yet some nights I felt I wanted to stay up there forever, to never have to drop back into reality.

Sometimes the most satisfying moments were to be found in the most hostile conditions. When there was nothing to see, other senses took over. It reminded me of the privilege I had in walking across Mull with one of the most remarkable people I had ever met. Michael Anderson was 75, blind and hard of hearing. I was a guide for part of his 16-day journey across Scotland, and I would give him a running commentary on the landscape as we went. I asked him what pleasure he got from walking when he lacked vision or sound. He told me he loved the feeling of the different levels of sun, rain and wind on his face, and how he could tell where he was by footfall. The whole experience has made me look at the landscape in a totally fresh way ever since.

When I reached the summit of Ben Hope to bring the year to a close in late December, it felt like a watershed moment. I realised that from now on, my moonwalking adventures will be different. These long dark nights in blizzards and gale-force winds may have proved to be among some of the hardest walks I have done, but they haven't put me off entirely. The night walks will become more of a treat than a main course, something to be savoured on long, clear nights, served with weather conditions that come with a guarantee. And I won't necessarily need a full moon as a dinner guest.

I may not have seen the whole of the moon, but it felt I came pretty close.

Glossary

Chapter 1

Beinn Alligin (Ben Ahligin) Mountain of beauty or jewelled mountain
Coir nan Laogh (Corra nan loo-ee) Corrie of the calf
Na Rathanan (Na Rahnan) The Horns (pulleys)
Sgurr Mhor (Skoor Voar) Big peak
Toll a' Mhadaidh Mhor (Toal a' Vatty Voar) Big hollow of the dog (can be wolf, fox)
Tom na Gruagaich (Toam na Groo-agich) Maiden's knoll

Chapter 2

Cairn Gorm (Cairn Gorram) Blue mountain
Coire an t-Sneachda (Corra an trechka) Corrie of the snows
Fiacaill a' Choire Chais (Fee-achil a' corra cas) Tooth of the steep corrie
Monadh Ruadh (Monna Roo-a) Red mountains

Chapter 3

Beinn a' Bheithir (Ben a' Vay-hir) Mountain of the thunderbolt (could also be serpent)
Creag Meagaidh (Craik Meggy) Bogland crag
Sgorr Dhonuill (Skorr Ghonill) Donald's peak
Sgorr Dearg (Skorr Jerrak) Red peak

Chapter 4

Bla Bheinn (Blah-ven) Blue mountain
Coire Uaigneich (Corra Oo-aignich) Lonely or remote corrie
Druim na Sgriodain (Drum na Screetan) Ridge of the screes

Chapter 5

Beinn Eighe (Ben Ay) File mountain
Coire Mhic Fhearchair (Corra Veechk Errachar) MacFarquhar's corrie
Liathach (Lee-aach) The grey place
Ruadh-stac Mor (Roo-a Stack Moar) Big red stack
Sgurr na Fearstaig (Skoor na Fyarstik) Peak of the thrift
Sgurr Fuar-thuill (Skoor Oo-ar Hoo-il) Peak of the cold hollow
Spidean Coire nan Clach (Speejan corra nan clach) Peak of the stony corrie

Chapter 6

An Teallach (An Chellach) The Forge
Ben Lawers (as spelled) Mountain of the loud stream
Beinn Ghlas (Ben Glass) Green mountain
Coire Odhair (Corra Oa-r) Dun-coloured corrie

Chapter 7

Beinn Fhionnlaidh (Ben Hee-only) Finlay's mountain
Carn Eighe (Carn Ay) Cairn of the notch
Mam Sodhail (Mam Soal) Hill of the barns
Mullach na Dheiragain (Moolach na Yerrakan) Summit of the kestrels
Sgurr nan Ceathreamhnan (Skoor nan Kerranan) Peak of the quarters

Chapter 8

Beinn a' Bhuiridh (Benn a' Voo-ry) Hill of the bellowing (of stags)
Beinn nan Aighenan (Ben nan Yanan) Hill of the hinds
Creag Coire na Fiar Bhealaich (Craik Corra na Fee-ar

Vyalich) Crag of the corrie of the slanting pass
Fionn Bheinn (Fee-on Ven) White hill
Gairich (Gaw-reech) Roaring (of stags)
Gleouraich (Glyawrich) Peak of roaring (of stags)
Sgurr a' Mhaoraich (Skoor a' Voerich) Peak of the shellfish
Sgurr Eilde Mor (Skoor Ailja Moar) Big peak of the hind
Sgurr na Ciche (Skoor na Keesha) Peak of the breast
Spidean Mialach (Speejan Mee-alach) Peak of deer
Stob Diamh (Stop Daff) Peak of the stag

Chapter 9

A' Chralaig (Chrah-lik) The Creel
Ben Cruachan (Ben Croo-achan) Conical mountain
Ben Starav (Ben Starrav) Bold mountain
Luinne Bheinn (Loon-ya Ven) Sea swelling hill

Chapter 10

A' Mhaighdean (Va-ijan) The Maiden
Beinn a' Ghlo (Ben a' Ghloe) Hill of the veil or mist
Beinn a' Chleidheimh (Ben a' Chlayva) Hill of the sword
Braigh Coire Chruinn-bhalgain (Bray Corra Chroo-in-valakin) Height of the corrie of round blisters
Carn Liath (Carn Lee-a) Grey hill
Mullach Coire Mhic Fhearchair (Moolach Corra Vhic Errachar) Summit of the corrie of Farquhar's son

Chapter 11

Aonach Dubh (Enach Doo) Black ridge
Beinn Mheadhoin (Ben Vane) Middle hill
Cac Carn Beag (Cachk Carn Bake) Little shit cairn
Coir' a' Ghrunnda (Corra a' Grunda) Floored corrie
Lochnagar (Loch-na-gaire) Loch of the noise

Sgurr nan Conbhairean (Skoor nan Connaviren) Peak of the dog-men
Sgurr Sgumain (Skoor Skooman) Mound peak

Chapter 12

Beinn a' Chlachain (Ben a' Chlachan) Mountain of the church hamlet
Beinn Sgritheall (Ben Scree-al) Mountain of screes
Druim Fada (Drum Atta) Long ridge
Ladhar Bheinn (Larven) Hoof-shaped mountain
Sgurr a' Gharaidh (Skoor a' Garry) Peak of the cave or den

Chapter 13

Ben Hope (Ben Hop) Hill of the bay

Acknowledgements

THE name on the front cover may be mine, but there are so many people who have provided help and support in so many ways during the walking, research, writing and production of this book. And like any big production, it's only when the credits roll at the end that you realise just how many have contributed.

Those who walked with me were rewarded with either stunning full moon nights and multi-coloured sunrises, or with the darkest of nights and challenging conditions. Many went out of their way to take part, and that I am eternally grateful. I like walking solo, but the more the year wore on, the more I was happy to have company.

In order of appearance then, big thanks to Andy Savage and Rebecca Ricketts; the BBC *Landward* team – Dougie Vipond, Susan Hendry, Kirsty McLaughlin, David Williamson; Pauline McEachen and James Millar; Patrick Baker; Robert Melvin and Susan Lunn; Rachael Ashdown and *The Scots Magazine* team, Rob Wight and Katrina Patrick; Eileen O'Neil, Andy Thow, Pauline McEachen (again) and Katrina Patrick (again).

Thanks also to those who provided support in so many different ways: Anne Butler, Cameron McNeish, Debby Waldron, Joan Lamb, The Grampian Club and its members, The Munro Society, *The Great Outdoors* magazine and *The Scots Magazine*, and all those who follow the *Moonwalker* blogs and pictures on social media. Special thank-you to Carol and Tracy at Tongue Hostel for their fabulous hospitality, and allowing me to use the hostel as a recording studio at short notice. Nothing was too much trouble for them. The staff at Good Spirits Company in Glasgow should also get a mention for their help in spending time helping me discover some interesting and unusual alcohol choices.

I suppose I should also mention the usual suspects: Martin Greig and Neil White at BackPage for their professionalism; Hugh MacDonald, for his usual careful word checking and moral support; cover designer Chris Hannah for his constant ideas and patience, and MBM Print, who ensured once again that this was a wholly Made in Scotland effort.

Alan Rowan
July 2019

About the Author

Alan Rowan is a writer, journalist, mountaineer and occasional film star. His first book, *Moonwalker: Adventures of a Midnight Mountaineer* was published by BackPage Press in 2014. The second Moonwalker book, *A Mountain Before Breakfast*, was published in 2016.

He has completed the Munros three times and is closing in on a fourth finish. He has also climbed the Furths (England, Wales and Ireland 3000ft peaks) and the Corbetts, and is fast approaching a Full House with a Grahams, Donalds and Munro Tops finish scheduled for later in 2019. He lives in Carnoustie on Scotland's sunny east coast.

More information, including mountain blogs, videos, photos and hill guides can be found at: www.munromoonwalker.com

You can check out the full *Mountains of the Moon* picture album by logging in to the Photography page at http://munromoonwalker.com/gallery

Facebook: www.facebook.com/MunroMoonwalker
Twitter @MunroMoonwalker
Instagram: MunroMoonwalker

MOONWALKER

ADVENTURES OF A MIDNIGHT MOUNTAINEER

ALAN ROWAN

For Alan Rowan there were always too many mountains and too little time. Then late none night, as he finished work at a national newspaper, he had a crazy idea; why not start the climb now, see the sun rise at 3,000 feet, and then come down the mountain while everyone else was getting out of bed?

See Alan's transformation from desk jockey to death-defying midnight mountaineer; meet rabid sheepdogs, charging deer, Victorian ghosts and talking trees – all the while taking in Scotland in a unique light.

Moonwalker is adventurous, funny and touching; at once a deeply personal memoir and unique travelogue.

FROM THE AUTHOR OF
"MOONWALKER"

A MOUNTAIN
BEFORE
BREAKFAST

ALAN ROWAN

The Munros may have been completed, but that doesn't mean the passion for night ascents of Scotland's mountains has been diminished for Alan Rowan. Fresh from seven years of nocturnal peak-bagging in *Moonwalker*, Alan now has his sights set on a new mountain list – the Corbetts.

Cue more midnight dashes across the country and more tales of madness and mayhem. There's car crashes and roads that don't exist; wild pigs and staring goats; the temporary loss of both feet; supermodel posties, giant chickens and snake-infested hillsides.

It's a tall order, but these mountains are going to be climbed – with or without Sandra Bullock.